Praise fo

Through her incredible writing, Jackie genuinely and selflessly shares the raw details of her journey with autoimmune encephalitis. As the father of an AE survivor, I understand the common feelings of loneliness and emptiness in not having anywhere to turn in such an unrelatable disease. I have cried along with strangers, and I shed tears while turning the pages of *Unwillable*. *Unwillable* will help those suffering through loneliness and give them hope. While we're making strides to identify and treat AE, it's not happening fast enough. The best we have right now is hope. And Jackie's story brings hope. The AE world needs Jackie, and it needs *Unwillable*.

William Gavigan, father of an AE survivor and Chairman of the Autoimmune Encephalitis Alliance

Unwillable is a brave and powerful book. Jackie Stebbins, a brilliant, driven young lawyer, wife, and mother, shares the devastating story of her illness with autoimmune encephalitis, a rare autoimmune brain disease, and her amazing recovery. As the mother of a son with autoimmune encephalitis, I found our story in Jackie's story. Jackie vividly describes her journey so that we experience what it feels like to descend into this rare illness's terror, pain, and uncertainty. Like Jackie, our son was cared for by Dr. McKeon at Minnesota's Mayo Clinic. Reading about Jackie's Mayo trip brought back to me the feelings of relief, hope, and grief that we felt when we went to Mayo and found a doctor who said, "I know what is wrong; we can treat the illness, and it will take a very, very long time to recover." In her book, Jackie shows us how she found the way through this darkness and how she found the way forward into a new life–a brilliant woman, wife, mother, and advocate who is showing other people who face autoimmune encephalitis how to "keep standing." I am grateful to be an autoimmune encephalitis warrior with Jackie!

Helen Egger MD, co-founder of the Autoimmune Encephalitis Alliance

In *Unwillable*, Jackie Stebbins takes you through her harrowing battle with autoimmune encephalitis. Piecing together her own story from memory, medical records, interviews and the handwritten journals she kept during her illness, Stebbins shines a light on a little-known and even less understood medical condition. In documenting her descent into illness and road to recovery, she pulls her readers into her story as she tries to first find out what's wrong with her and then find out what that diagnosis *actually* means, not just medically but for her life going forward. Stebbins engages readers through the unflinching honesty, attention to detail and palpable willpower that she displays both in facing her illness and in her storytelling.

Maria Burns Ortiz, co-author NYT bestseller *My Fight/Your Fight*

This wonderful book tells the wrenching true story of Jackie Stebbins, a rising legal star in North Dakota, whose career was cruelly cut short by a little-known disease, Autoimmune Encephalitis. The book—conceived as she began to see hope of recovery rather than expectation of imminent death—takes the reader on a rollercoaster of emotions. It is a gripping story, analogous to a legal/medical thriller. I found it sometimes painful to read about the impacts of this dreadful disease on Jackie's body, mind and spirit, but it is also inspiring and hopeful.

Through Jackie's exquisite unsparing writing, we see how she progressed from being a farm kid in far southwest North Dakota to becoming one of North Dakota's best and most successful lawyers and a rising political star at a very young age. We see how she built the life for which she had worked so hard (dream house, loving husband and children, dream car, co-owner of a thriving law firm). And then we share her suffering as she abruptly lost her health, her law career, and why she feared -- realistically -- she would even lose her life. We almost stop breathing as we follow her painful journey and her belated discovery that her crises were due to an undiagnosed Autoimmune Encephalitis. Jackie's writing will make readers weep with shared sympathy, but it will also make readers celebrate as she explains how she eventually achieved recovery with the support of insightful medical practitioners, the support of her family and friends and her own phenomenal courage and faith in God.

Jackie Stebbins takes the reader through the details of the most important trial this young lawyer ever faced. This was a trial about her health, and the verdict could be life or death. Her own! This book allows you to understand how and why this courageous young woman never gave up, and how she survived a devastating challenge. You will read the last page and feel an uplifting spirit about the remarkable Jackie Stebbins.

Jackie's story challenges us to think about what we would do if everything that we built, personally and professionally was suddenly and dramatically taken away. Would we meet the challenges with Jackie's perseverance and determination to discover the truth? We are reminded in these pages that if you have your health, you have everything, and also if you have a loving family, you can survive any challenge.

UNWILLABLE

This book has been donated to Overlook Ridge Library by Ruth Kline — Grandmother of author Jackie M. Stebbins

June 2022

Wisdom
Editions

Minneapolis

First Edition May 2022
UNWILLABLE: A Journey to Reclaim My Brain.
Copyright © 2022 by Jackie M. Stebbins. All rights reserved.

Printed in the United States of America.
10 9 8 7 6 5 4 3 2 1
ISBN: 978-1-950743-81-0

Cover art and design by Lacie J. Van Orman
Book interior design by Gary Lindberg
Author photograph (back cover) by Jesse Knutson Photography

To my parents, who inspired my possible
To my husband, who allows my possible
To my children, for everything's possible

No star is ever lost we once have seen,
We always may be what we might have been

–Adelaide Anne Procter

Table of Contents

UNWILLABLE

A Journey to Reclaim My Brain

Jackie M. Stebbins

Wisdom
Editions
Minneapolis

Author's Note

The illness that prompted me to write this memoir gave me amnesia, so most of the climax of this book comes from my reconstructing events. I obtained much of the information by interviewing my husband and mother and a few close friends. I was also aided by medical records, emails, my journals, and my work calendar. I did not take artistic license in the re-creation.

Foreword

Writing a book is a huge achievement on both a personal and a professional level. Whilst perhaps more common these days than it once was, it is still something that most people will not achieve in their lifetime.

You might wonder to yourself why you should be in awe of a well-educated lawyer writing a book. I would like to tell you.

By itself, writing a book is an incredible achievement, but in this case the author had teetered on what was suspected to be the brink of madness only to realise the abyss into which she peered was in fact, perhaps more daunting, a neurological condition of which learned only a couple decades ago and for which we are still conducting trials. Perhaps more worrisome is its high death rate (up to 40 percent dependent on cause[1]) and a relapse rate of between 12 and 35 percent[2] (dependent on cause).

---

1   Schubert J, Brämer D, Huttner HB, Gerner ST, Fuhrer H, Melzer N, Dik A, Prüss H, Ly LT, Fuchs K, Leypoldt F, Nissen G, Schirotzek I, Dohmen C, Bösel J, Lewerenz J, Thaler F, Kraft A, Juranek A, Ringelstein M, Sühs KW, Urbanek C, Scherag A, Geis C, Witte OW, Günther A; GENERATE and IGNITE network. Management and prognostic markers in patients with autoimmune encephalitis requiring ICU treatment. Neurol Neuroimmunol Neuroinflamm. 2018 Oct 30;6(1):e514. https://doi:10.1212/NXI.0000000000000514 . PMID: 30568992; PMCID: PMC6278855.

2   Dalmau J, Graus F. Antibody-Mediated Encephalitis. N Engl J Med. 2018 Mar 1;378(9):840-851. https://doi:10.1056/NEJMra1708712 . PMID: 29490181.

To crawl back from this terror, to continue raising your children, loving your husband, and yet facing the paradox of losing everything you had ever worked for including a thriving law business, not to mention your mind at one point, is no mean feat.

People who have been affected by encephalitis often suffer great losses. You don't see it coming. One day you are perfectly fine and the next you are in a hospital waking from a coma, or in Jackie's case entering psychiatric pathways because you have a condition eight out of ten people around the world have never heard of[3]. A condition by the way, that is more common in many countries than ALS, multiple sclerosis, bacterial meningitis, and cerebral palsy—conditions which have much higher public and clinical profiles.

If you survive, you are met with bewildered looks when you try to describe your problems and what you have been through. Not just because the people you are speaking to have never heard of it but because in most cases you look just fine. Another cruel paradox of this condition is you can't see a broken brain.

These are just a few of the issues people affected by encephalitis face. But, when you put them all together, it often results in people not understanding why you aren't getting yourself together more quickly given that you look fine. The result is often a constant battle to get back to who and where you were, because you don't understand why you can't.

Broken brains take a long time to heal, if they heal at all. As this battle continues, many people face repeated failures to return to work and education. Their mental health can suffer, and, in some cases, families break down. With all this comes a loss of confidence so great, that you are often unable to believe that you will ever achieve anything again. And some survivors succumb to the black dog of depression and neglect.

So, what Jackie has done is not only run the gauntlet of this often-devastating condition—encephalitis—but she then set herself the additional marathon of writing this book.

---

3 Easton, A. (2019). What is encephalitis? The Biomedical Scientist: https://the-biomedicalscientist.net/science/what-encephalitis

Why? Well, it's simple. Writing your story can help you understand what has happened to you. This is especially true at times when not many things are making sense. Jackie has always been a high achiever, pushing herself to the limit and sometimes to her detriment, beyond. Jackie was motivated by the goal to understand her own journey to share her story so others would not feel so alone and might find solace, hope and perhaps inspiration from her experience.

I met Jackie on social media (it is good for some things!), and as a result, Jackie and I bonded and became friends. It is my honour to write this foreword to her book. I commend it to you and hope that you will find something in it that might comfort or motivate you.

Dr Ava Easton (PhD)
April 2021
www.encephlaitis.info
@encephalitisava

Prologue

I was a thirty-three-year-old trial lawyer, self-employed by my own law firm, when it all began. With the benefit of hindsight, it started in the fall of 2017. That year overwhelmed me like none other, and it seemed like I was always trying to catch my breath. I felt like I barely made it through. And then the world came crashing down in May 2018, when I was diagnosed with autoimmune encephalitis, a serious and rare brain disease that I had never heard of. For months, it took my mind and body as prisoners. It nearly killed me.

But, by nothing short of a miracle, I was correctly diagnosed and quickly treated. And, although I made a triumphant recovery, it has left plenty of aftereffects in my life. My world was forever changed, and it happened nearly overnight.

Unwillable is the story of a small-town North Dakota farm girl who achieved her wildest dreams as a successful lawyer. At only thirty-four years old, she ran a successful practice as a family law and criminal defense attorney and owned a million-dollar law firm. She was at the height of her career and was building her life and a future for her family when she was diagnosed with autoimmune encephalitis. She thought the disease would take it all away from her—but it didn't.

She rose to the challenge. She survived. She recovered. She rebuilt. This is a story of survival through devastation. This story is mine.

* * *

What is your biggest fear? What truly scares you the most? In college, I would have answered, being attacked while walking alone. In law school, an easy answer, failing the bar exam. As a young attorney, the fear of committing malpractice gave me great concern. But in 2017, if you would have asked me those questions, I believe I would have had four answers: anything bad happening to my children, either me or my husband dying young and leaving our children, the loss of my husband Sean, and losing my career.

I've now heard the saying "Run to your fears and they will disappear," but I don't think I had ever heard that in 2017. I never wanted to face my greatest fears, as I hoped I could get through life without having to do so. But because I'm human and know my time on earth is finite, there was something inside of me that made me ponder my existence. It was something that said *What's going to happen to me? What will be the tragedy in my life?* As I aged and saw cancer claim the lives of many around me, I wondered if it would be cancer. But deep down, I think I knew that wasn't it. Honestly, something told me cancer wasn't strange enough for me.

After graduating law school, I began to worry about hurting my head. I had put nearly $100,000 of student loans into my brain and hoped to have a profitable career, so I was fearful of it being harmed. When I began my first job in private practice, I started wearing a bike helmet when I rode and purchased life insurance.

When I started my own law firm, I bought disability and cancer insurance and felt some peace of mind. But I became very afraid of losing my career and spoke openly with my law partner about my fear of getting too sick to work, but not enough to die. Looking back, those conversations seem like eerie premonitions. Wearing a bike helmet was one thing, but relying on insurance to protect me from serious disability or death was another.

The fact that I was so preoccupied with my head and mortality then seems surreal now. After all, when I began to seriously prepare for the worst, I was only thirty-one years old and in overall good health.

Run to your fears and they will disappear. I didn't run to my fears, but in 2018 I stood face-to-face with some of my darkest fears. It was straight out of a horror story. For months I lay at the threshold of hell as the devil himself stood over me. Something happened to me, and it almost took me away from my husband and kids. It took away my career. It injured my brain. It had a slow and terrorizing onset. It wasn't even something I knew by name. And it was scarier than I ever could have imagined.

PART I—AND SO IT ALL BEGINS

Oh, I've finally decided my future lies
Beyond the yellow brick road.

"Goodbye Yellow Brick Road" by Elton John

CHAPTER 1

When I finally landed in the psychiatric ward on the evening of May 14, 2018, I had many more questions than answers. I was there because I begged to be, and I believed it would be the place to deliver me from my insomnia. The protracted period of sleepless nights was debilitating, and the ensuing effects had become unbearable. The tremors that had begun in my hands had moved throughout my entire body. White noise blared in my ears in a constant loop. The exhaustion had depleted my spirit and my being. There was almost nothing left of me but incessant, wet sobs.

I have some memories from my forty-eight-hour voluntary commitment, but they don't really feel like memories. To me, memories are images and stories that you can hold on to and share. Reflecting on those two days conjures up more feelings than recollections. My memories are more like pictures—some moving, like a brief video, some still. I can picture the clock on the bare wall in my room, jumping around when I look at its face. I can see my shaking hand, trying desperately to write the date, as I sat on my small bed with the thin, white sheets. There's my friend, Father Chris, wearing his purple stole, waiting to hear my teary and radical confession in the cluttered room we sat in. I watch the open space where people gather and eat. All the patients around me are eating at long tables in their red scrubs. Every patient is in red, except for me. I see a group session in a room with a closed door. We're sitting in hospital chairs, basic wooden ones with maroon, cloth seats and backs, at a rectangular table. I can't see the group, but I can see an older woman with a stiff face and black hair, crying, but she makes little sound. I can't smell anything. The usual sterile hospital smells of disinfectant, sanitizer, rubber gloves, and bad food escape me. Yet the entire place is antiseptic; it has no feel or vibe. It's a place where you're just there, but no one wants to be there. In my wildest notions, I never would have guessed I'd end up there. But I was there… alone.

The whole experience flashes at me in shards of blur and bright lights. But I can still feel the fear. The despair. I can barely sense that slight sliver of hope, even though my life had begun to feel hopeless. I can feel myself nearing the end. I know that it all goes black when I leave the psychiatric ward.

While my complete stay isn't embedded in my memory, because of what the illness was doing to my brain, my time there will never be forgotten because of its place in my life's story. That experience definitively marks where I'm right at the edge between a well-educated, successful, driven, independent, and thriving woman and an incapacitated person, powerless and relegated to the care of those around her, on the brink of brain damage or death without the intervention of the correct diagnosis. And a small part of me now believes I then understood that I was teetering on a life-altering and explosive line. But that same small part of me can't say whether, for the first time in my life, I believed my situation to be unwillable. Perhaps my own will would not be enough.

I will always remember crawling into bed the first night, ragged with emotion, and the racing thoughts my mind was still able to conjure up. The questions pulsed through my silent tears. *What the hell happened to me? I'm only thirty-four years old. I have a husband and two beautiful children. I cannot possibly belong here. I haven't led a life that would lead me to this dysfunction. I was doing so well. I have a home in a cul-de-sac. I am a well-respected trial lawyer. I'm the senior partner at my law firm. I've never before had a problem with mental health. My life was full of happiness. God, I was so funny. I loved making people laugh. Why now and why is it so serious? Why am I so desperate for help? Why am I at rock bottom? How the hell did I end up in a psychiatric ward?*

* * *

When people ask me what I was like when I was young, I reply, "The same, only shorter." I was an energetic and humorous little person. I was also a tomboy, with my own sense of style. One of the best depictions of my young personality is my favorite childhood photograph that I found at my grandma's house. I'm three and a half years old, riding my beat-up tricycle on our gravel driveway. I'm wearing a little red and blue sweater with skyscrapers on the front... and worn-out shoes. A turtle backpack hugs my shoulders, and binoculars hang around my neck. Completing the outfit was my dirty, red "Tom's Auto Body" hat. That hat became notorious because I never left the house without it, including when I wore it with a dress at a cousin's wedding in Denver. My face says, "I may get into trouble, but watch this." If only I could remember the purpose of my mission that day.

I've always been ready to go, to do something big in my own unique way. In 1984, in the dead of a freezing plains winter, my parents traveled the dark, open highway for forty-five miles and barely made it to the hospital for my birth. Dad didn't even get his coat off before I appeared. I was born independent.

I was raised on my family's small farm, outside of the rural town of Bowman, in the sparsely populated, homogenous state of North Dakota. While growing up, I hated living on a farm. I believed my existence to be dull. I watched a lot of old VHS movies and wondered what life felt like when you weren't so bored; in a place where you didn't live miles away from a town of one thousand people and had more than three television channels; where the long winters didn't keep you cooped up at your home, without sidewalks, streetlights, and next-door friends. That and we didn't have the means to create much excitement. I can still recall the conversation when I was about ten, and I asked Dad if we were in the middle class. It was more of a request for an affirmation than it was a question. He replied, "No, according to our taxes, we're poor." That wasn't a subtle nuance either. Dad's sweet, but blunt. It was fairly obvious given life around us, but it was hard for young me to accept.

I then swore that when I got older I would never live on a farm nor in a small town, and I wouldn't ever be poor. And while I was fiercely proud of the tiniest part of the world I occupied, the angst nearly boiled out of me over the years. I wanted so much more than Bowman had to offer. I couldn't tolerate everyone and their dog knowing every detail about my life. While a junior in high school, I crawled out of a window at a party to avoid the unwelcomed cops who showed up. Along with two friends, we ran in the dark hills for what became a long night. It was by far the most rogue thing I had ever done. When I got to the town café early the next morning for my serving job, a local asked me if I needed to borrow his coat for a quick run outside. In a small town, everything about your life is open to speculation and gossip. And it's hard to be on the fringes. That same year, I supported Al Gore for president, along with my classmate, Leo. We were outnumbered thirty-two to two. Our odds were not unique to the county or state. I wanted out.

I escaped some through movies, but mostly it was through John Grisham. After I read my first Grisham novel, *The Client*, in fifth grade, I continued to read all he had to offer for years, and my life's path felt solidified. I would be a fancy lawyer. I would live in an exciting big city with entertainment and anonymity. And I could buy all the things I wanted. Like a purple BMW.

Of course, I was a kid, and I had a lot to learn about life. We may have led a simple life on the farm, but it was a good life. During much of the '80s and '90s, my parents struggled greatly. They persevered through drastic weather patterns and meager financial benefit, yet always remained steadfast in their desire to give us a happy childhood in our rural place. Looking back, they gave me everything I needed and more. No one ever hurt me, and we always had a home and health insurance. We were well fed, celebrated holidays and birthdays, enjoyed time with extended family, and were active in our community. My parents were both college-educated and committed to our education, work ethic, and faith in the Catholic Church. We were expected to attend mass without fail. After staying out all night after my junior prom, I sat in the back church pew with my best friend, Lacie, and picked bobby pins out of my hair while following along in prayer.

With time, I realized that the people in Bowman are some of the most heartfelt, supportive, and generous people I've ever met, even if our politics generally differ. A lot of people knew the details of my life, because they cared. From preschool to senior graduation, I hardly had a teacher I didn't enjoy and respect. Our community was safe and very rarely made headline news. People wanted so much for me, and I knew it. I had a fortunate upbringing.

* * *

I'm the middle child of three, born in 1984. I often complained about the oppression of being stuck between two brothers, to the point where Dad worried that I'd engrave on his headstone, "I never had a car like him." I look a lot like both of my siblings and have been confused as a twin to each one. We all have dark hair and bold brown eyes, and we are all the same nominal height. But we're wired quite differently.

My older brother, Mike, has a master's degree in engineering, and he's one of the smartest people I know. I realized how exceptionally intelligent he was when people were buying and selling his high school precalculus notebook long after he graduated. David, my younger brother who has a business degree, is also good with numbers. And problem solving comes naturally as a result of his many years of working on farms, ranches, and North Dakota's booming oil fields. Mike is quieter and more reserved, and David is wry. I usually laugh a lot with David, but it's hard because I'm frequently on the receiving end of his quick wit.

The way we look mostly comes from my dad, Jack. Dad is a farmer turned real estate broker. He is smart, quiet, and fiercely brave. He's battled muscular dystrophy, a heart attack, and kidney failure, but if you ask how he's doing, he answers, "Fine." He's had a moustache my entire life, except for when he shaved it off the day after my wedding to shock us all. Dad is reserved, but he's not without wit.

I furiously cling to Dad's Italian genetics. His heritage gave me the gifts of being stubborn, carrying a grudge, and talking with my hands. My short, but mighty, Italian great-aunt nearly poked your eyes out when she spoke. That skipped Dad's generation and went straight to me. I'm very animated and social, but I get that from Mom.

My blond mother, Colleen, is my hero. She gave us our pale skin and the desire to look words up in a dictionary and use proper grammar. She was always my parent first, but as I grew toward adulthood we became best friends. She is remarkably kind and never judgmental, which made her a wonderful public health nurse for nearly forty years. She had to be, to teach puberty classes and take care of head lice in our rural place. Her faith in God and family are powerful, and she never carries grudges. She gets that from my saintly grandmother. She inherited my grandfather's wit, but I inherited his wit combined with storytelling and attention seeking. When I work a room and command an audience, that's straight out of his act. Grandpa had endless stories and jokes to tell and made people feel welcome. It wasn't until I was older that I could fully appreciate my draw to his personality.

I began speaking in full sentences when I was one year old and haven't taken a lot of breaths since. At an early age, I became adept at arguing to get my way. One time, while standing in the kitchen in my underwear and purple jelly shoes, I became incredulous at the empty vitamin bottle. I placed my hands on my hips and seriously stated to Mom, "Well, this is just ridiculous." I often used aphorisms, but incorrectly. I once told my first-grade teacher, "Don't lay your eggs before they hatch." I also defined exaggeration to her, Grandpa's famous trait, as telling a story and "juicing it up."

When I was only four years old, my antics led Mom to wryly write that my parents threatened me that I had to stop manipulating them and trying to bargain with them, or that Social Services would take *them* away. It was only natural that I would want to be a lawyer. The arguing and my memory. I began memorizing license plates in my small town because quite a few of my friends drove a similar red Pontiac. And in a small town where you drove on Main Street for fun, it was important to me to be able to differentiate. Whether out of boredom or to test myself, I then began memorizing as many of the license plates around me as I could. I hoped it would lead me to working in the FBI or CIA. When I was fourteen, I sent away for information on joining the FBI and found out that the best way in was to become an attorney or an accountant. All roads always led me back to becoming a lawyer.

I loved school and was known to entertain there. I was often seen and always heard. Many parent-teacher conferences began with, "Jackie is a good student, but she talks a lot." I got into less trouble for it as I got older because the teachers were all used to me, and they appreciated me. I was kind, a natural leader, and I aided the underdogs. I've always had little time for people who make others feel insecure or unworthy. My defense of others was displayed on the playground and in the lunchroom long before I was in a courtroom. I still enjoy taking in outcasts and, as an attorney, love a good fight for someone on the margins. I think it's because I fit in so well, and carry on conversations with such ease, that I worry about others who don't share that talent. I'm told that I'm very inclusive and make people comfortable, mostly with my self-deprecating humor.

I've always felt very fortunate to have a lot of friends and the ability to get along well with most everyone. I've never been much for small cliques. I enjoy having a vast network of people around me. I routinely find myself doing things outside the norm. In college, I laughed along as a guy mocked me to the whole history class because he said I wrote in "'80's cursive." It didn't faze me much, just reminded me that I'm an anomaly. I had been writing exclusively in cursive since I learned how in third grade, and I thought everyone else did too. Printing always felt mundane.

Out of all the memories in my vault, something that sticks with me from childhood is from fourth grade, when I first remember having anxiety about sleep. I was definitely the kid who couldn't stay over at a friend's house, and if I tried I usually ended up with a late-night stomachache. If I couldn't fall asleep on a school night, I fretted, and the more I fretted, the less able I was to relax and go to sleep. It routinely happened on Sunday nights. It began with my family winding down around the television to the ticking clock on CBS's 60 Minutes. That sound was the first stark reminder that Monday lay ahead. After dinner and any schoolwork, I was off to bed not too far from the living room. If I could later hear my parents watching the television sitcoms *M*A*S*H* or *Cheers* while I was still lying awake, I knew it was past my bedtime. I then worried about being tired the next day. And if Mom and Dad went to bed while I still lay awake in the quiet, dark house, I got a sick feeling in my stomach.

The Sunday night's sleep anxiety became a pattern for me, even as an adult. But as long as it was only Sunday night, I dealt with it. I also wore myself out as I aged. I became a busy and tired teenager and a college and law student who juggled school, activities, and work. I was notorious for being rundown and sick with colds and sinus infections. When I began lawyering and added children into the equation, I was stretched so thin that I felt eternally exhausted. Yet, deep down, I always believed being drained was better than struggling to sleep because I never really forgot the scary sounds and feelings of Sunday nights that had begun at a young age.

I managed my fear of not sleeping until true insomnia struck, and it was scarier than I ever imagined. In 2018, I was in my mid-thirties when I became a depressed insomniac. Or so I thought. And I could no longer write in cursive.

CHAPTER 2

I want so much to be relaxed and easygoing, but I struggle with an intense and focused personality that tries to dominate anything I do. I don't remember ever being anything other than very driven. Like in eighth grade when I decided that I wanted to win the state free throw competition and not just participate like in years past. I shot hundreds of free throws a day and did it the same, serious way—every single time. At State, I made twenty-three for twenty-five free throws, and won. In college, I met a girl named Ashley who realized she had competed against me at the state tournament. It was years later, but she remembered how confidently I had stepped up to the line and how I was laser focused.

In my limited athletic glory days when I was younger, I pushed myself hard. I loved competition. I constantly fed my personality. It helped me stay busy and gave me some meaning in my small place, but mostly I felt a strong desire to look "perfect." With cross-training, I believed I could engineer a "perfect body." Year round, I ran, biked, lifted weights, and swam nearly every day. I also kickboxed and became a black belt in Taekwondo.

Along with getting me through my high school angst, I felt empowered by my self-discipline. I had genuine faith that my own willpower and dedication would get me anywhere I wanted to go. I could always be as successful as I drove myself to be. I knew I would need that focus to get through law school, so I never believed that I could actually use my drive to hurt myself, or that my workouts could be counterproductive.

And I definitely didn't obtain a perfect body, whatever that was. Between my genetic chicken legs and my bulky arms and back, I began to look like a lady powerlifter, and that was not the look I desired. When I tried on a red dress from Victoria's Secret for my high school graduation, I looked at my back in the mirror... and started crying.

I "liked" to run as much as anyone I know "likes" to run, but I began running in high school. I loved gravel country roads. I enjoyed moving through the cool, wet springs, the early morning sky in the summer, and the sights and sounds of fall. But I sure didn't love the way the pounding always seemed to nag at my legs, especially when I used a treadmill during the long North Dakota winters. I doubt I ever went more than four miles. I had the discipline to run and felt its empowerment by pushing through sweat and side aches, but my body was not designed to run. I'm flat footed and suffer from serious overpronation. Custom orthotics mostly rectified the problems I had with my lower extremities and allowed me to stay very active through high school, but it wasn't healthy for me as I aged. Surely that didn't occur to me as a teen. I just thought I had bad luck and was prone to injury.

I've never met another woman who had Rocky Balboa-type shoulder injuries beginning in junior high, like me. I suffered quite a few shoulder mishaps from basketball until my right shoulder completely dislocated while I was swimming laps as a junior in high school. It was quite the sight to watch three people trying to drag me out of the pool with my right arm stuck straight up in the air. It took the lifeguard, who was the center of our basketball team, an EMT who just happened to also be swimming laps, and another nice lady. The EMT helped me to her car and drove me to the emergency room right down the street. I yelped as the automatic seat belt hooked my arm when she started the car, but we managed. After that episode, I hoped to keep that shoulder firmly in its socket. I mostly succeeded... until I was in college, and my bad luck struck again.

In February, during my junior year and only two nights before my twenty-first birthday, I was playing in a very physical intramural basketball game. Someone tripped me and I crashed down onto the floor, landing on my right shoulder. My screaming stopped the entire gym. It had dislocated again, and I spent my twenty-first birthday getting free pity drinks because of my sling.

I had the shoulder surgically repaired in July and recovered at home in Bowman. For four weeks my shoulder was in a sling that was belted to my waist, and it was painful. I studied for the LSAT sitting on my bed and, unable to run, walked endless miles on country roads. The physical therapy was arduous. I wasn't able to even lift my arm until months later, but I managed to wash my hair and drive with one arm. I believed that surgery was worth it because my shoulder would forever stay in its socket. But the aching aftermath remained, as pain radiated through my shoulder, neck, and back. It followed me that last year of college and during my marathons of sitting and reading during law school and in my profession.

By the time of surgery, my determination was an inherent problem. It was no longer good or bad luck. I drove myself too hard. People close to me encouraged me to slow down and hoped that I wasn't doing anything to cause myself pain or serious injuries. I assured them I wasn't, but I was deceiving them and myself. Some of my ways were destructive, but in my mind it was the way toward success. I felt the double standards and pressure women faced. I knew that I would need to be mentally tough to succeed in law school and as a lawyer. So I convinced myself that my way of grit, determination, and sacrifice was the only way. I learned how to tune people out when they questioned my methods and told myself to stay the course. I became polished at avoiding pain and red flags about my health and stayed on the same path of all-or-nothing thoughts toward my body.

I continued on, until the last time I tried to enjoy a carefree run and felt pain that never really went away. It was Friday, and I had just completed the horrific first year of law school. I jogged out to enjoy the warm May day and bask in having that dreaded year in the rear-view mirror. But, from that day on, lasting through most of my time in law school, my leg pain became a protracted saga of doctoring, tests, physical therapy, reduced activities, and unanswered questions.

My quadriceps and femurs were injured, and nothing seemed to heal them. Then a doctor told me in no uncertain terms that I was placing excessive demands upon my body. I needed to physically slow down and give myself, and my legs, a break. I was young and selfish, so I didn't like her and her opinion. I was hurt and felt misunderstood. But I begrudgingly realized I had to learn how to balance my life without using exercise as a drug to feed my obsessive and perfectionist personality. It was the precursor to the greater imbalance of my life... the noise in my head that I tried to dull and run from.

At the time, it felt like the end of my world. It became a phase in my life when I had to accept that I would never return to running or high impact sports. I fought my desire to control my body image and tried to find different ways to release my stress while on an intense path toward a stressful career. It was hard.

A few years into private practice, I began mending myself a great deal physically by resting my body and exercising more responsibly. I mostly turned to swimming, along with some walking and biking. I aqua jogged in the pool, which cleared my mind in the ways running had, yet left me with little pain. Swimming became my lifeline, even in the months when I had to drive to the pool in the darkness of early morning and freezing winter temps. As I healed, I swore I had learned my life's lesson about not pushing myself too hard. I thought I was listening better when people told me to slow down. But I had already begun channeling all my energy into my work because I believed it was the best move for me. I was blazing a new trail by concentrating on my career, to build a great life for me and the family I would have one day. I felt the control again but thought I could handle it.

I realize now that I never really changed my ways. I only changed my focus. Once my physical attributes were gone, I made unreasonable demands upon my work life. I couldn't compete physically anymore, so I competed mentally. I was back to proving myself in a game that no one else was playing. And it's why I believed that I caused myself to self-destruct at only thirty-four years old.

CHAPTER 3

Prior to my college orientation, I didn't give much thought to my major or what I would be good at because I was so preoccupied by law school. What I did eventually decide was that an out-of-state school seemed out of reach for me. By my junior year of high school, the reality of my limited finances had set in and told me to think local. And a powerful carrot dangled in front of me for a full-tuition scholarship at a state school because of a noble, local woman named Alyce Travers, who left the bulk of her estate for area students' higher education.

A close, older friend of mine assured me that the University of North Dakota (UND), located in the coldest, farthest corner of the state away from Bowman, had a reputable party scene and, most importantly for me, it had a law school. Between the promise of a full scholarship if I earned good grades, a law school to keep me focused, and some fun to be had, the decision to attend UND became an easy one. And while I never knew Alyce, I repeatedly looked to the heavens to thank her as she kept me extremely nervous about earning As and covered my tuition for four years.

As I sat bright-eyed on campus on a hot summer Monday morning, I was tasked with registering for my first semester of college while my parents sat through a video on student loan debt. Not only did I not have a major, I had no idea how to plan college courses and credits. Not wanting to seem too needy, I pretended that I fit right in. When a professor, who I later learned was beloved on campus and an attraction for the young females, quickly walked by me and questioned my major, I just spit it out, "Political Science." He then helped me pick a few general courses and carried on.

I already had a strong interest in the law, but after taking a trip to Washington, DC, as a senior in high school only months after 9-11, my interest in politics soared. I spent time with North Dakota's congressional delegation, and Senator Byron Dorgan allowed me and the one other North Dakota girl onto the Senate floor with him, where he introduced us to General Colin Powell. As I shook his hand, in awe of his large presence, I managed to mutter, "Nice to meet you, sir."

I assumed political science would be a good fit. I didn't know much about the discipline, but believed I'd learn along the way. I declared my major that day and never looked back.

The only other occupation I had ever considered was that of a motivational speaker. Sometime in high school, after I attended a conference with moving national speakers, I asked Mom how to pursue that path. She answered me gently. "Well, first you need to have a career and be good at something, and then you also need some type of special story." As it became apparent I couldn't study motivational speaking, and because I had neither a career nor a story, I catalogued her advice in the back of my mind. I then got started on my career, which I knew all began in college. But for many years thereafter, I dreamed of speaking to a big crowd and always went back to Mom's advice: first a career and then a story.

While in college, I was already no stranger to hard work. I knew I needed to study hard to earn As, and I knew I needed a job to help with expenses. Beginning in junior high, I babysat to purchase clothing and shoes I wanted, and all through high school I worked as a server to help support myself and feed my expensive Taekwondo habit. Once I got to college, I took a job at the local country club. I was experienced in the leers, demands, and fights with cooks that came as a young female in food service, but a private club was a world of its own. Some days I felt abused by members, but I enjoyed my coworkers and never desired to make minimum wage when I knew that my work ethic could earn me hundreds of dollars in tips in a single shift. It fit my personality of never settling for the minimum and always working harder to obtain the maximum.

While I studied tirelessly and worked nights and weekends, I still had an amazing college experience. I made many new friends, but I was lucky enough to stay close to my oldest friend from childhood, Lacie. Lacie and I became best friends in junior high. She drew me in by her quiet demeanor, her superior intellect, and her apathetic, dry wit. As we grew up, I realized that Lacie was the anti-Jackie, but that's what made us, well, *us*. We spent a lot of time together pulling pranks, rollerblading, and dreaming about life outside of our small town. We endlessly drove around in her old Pontiac. Her listening, me talking, and a lot of '90s music playing.

In college, she immersed in art, graphic design, and guitars in coffee shops. She sought to travel the world. I attended Democratic fundraisers and argued politics over beer. With my sights fixated on the university's law school and my pockets empty, I thought of going nowhere but down-campus for another three years. Yet we still saw a lot of each other. We laughed endlessly in joy, and I always looked to her first in both my sorrows and fears. Since the age of twelve, I have gone to her on all pressing matters in life. Lacie is a rock, and she'll always be *my* rock.

During my sophomore year of college, another lifelong friend came into the picture, and she had a North Dakota-famous last name. When I was in high school, Heidi Heitkamp was the state's attorney general, and she ran a remarkable race for governor. I was drawn to Heidi because she was a budding lawyer feminist's dream. So when I met her niece, Ashley, at my first presidential primary rally, I was mesmerized by what I saw as Ashley's fame and her strong personality. I sensed her take-charge attitude, albeit in a small frame. Ashley's about a half foot shorter than me. And at only 5'5" I'm not very tall, except in basketball when the coach said I was over 5'7", which threatened exactly no one.

We quickly became soul sisters. Between our same politics, similar interests, and parallel career paths, we spent a lot of time together. With her blond hair and my brown hair, our inseparability, and because it was 2003, many people dubbed us as the "Bush Twins." Some actually thought we were lesbians. We preferred the latter to the former. We eventually separated for a while when she went to law school in Wisconsin, and I stayed at UND, but we still remained close.

And, fortunately for me, I didn't have to spend too much time looking for Mr. Right in college because I had already found him.

While I was lucky to always have friends growing up, I never had any boyfriends. Until my husband, Sean, came along at just the wrong time and changed that for me.

Sean and I both have different versions of how we met, but it involves two weddings and a track meet. No matter the details of how it all worked out, it all seemed to work out… because we've been together ever since.

Sean is two years older than I am and grew up in a neighboring small town. He had done a year of radio college in Minneapolis, Minnesota, before moving back home to work. I was weeks away from graduating high school and purposefully remained unattached, just biding my time until I could swim in the larger dating pool in college. That and I never felt like guys were interested in me. It also didn't help when I was often told that guys were "afraid of me." They were only my buddies, and nothing more. My independence, assertion, and feminism, coupled with the black belt I trained for, were obvious problems. But I just felt homely.

Whether serendipity or my not paying attention, I didn't know Sean prior to his liquid courage at a wedding dance and the red and white outline of sunglasses on my face from a wind burn I sustained at a track meet. He claims to have noticed me from afar and felt an instant attraction. I think he's lying. I liked his build and radio voice, but he won me over with his humor.

Sean was different from other guys my age. He had a personality that everyone appreciated. He was funny, charming, and sweet. Everyone I knew loved Sean, and I quickly realized that I did too. It was unnerving for me because I was only eighteen, and I hadn't envisioned a boyfriend entering my life, but I immediately sensed his unending devotion to me. He met my family and hung out with my little brother. He also felt compelled to drive me fifty miles on gravel roads into the middle of nowhere to train with my favorite black belt because he feared I might get stranded with a flat tire. It annoyed me at first, but I accepted it because he wasn't saying I wasn't capable, just that he wanted to be there for me.

Whether I was immediately conscious of it or not, Sean radically accepted me. He wasn't threatened by me, didn't ask me to change who I was, and happily watched me chase my dreams. I couldn't believe such a man existed, but he was real.

We also respected each other as equals, with little care for traditional gender roles. He liked to cook, did his own laundry, and even before we had children offered to be a stay-at-home dad so I could work long hours. He reminded me of my father in the way he always stood beside me, just as Dad did Mom. We dated all through college, and when he didn't leave me during my crazed first year of law school, I knew it could work for a lifetime.

As Sean and I married during my third year of law school and embarked upon a wonderful life together, I never dreamed that I would need him in order to stay alive. Marrying Sean was quite possibly the best decision I ever made.

CHAPTER 4

I knew all the lawyer jokes going into law school, but I hadn't heard the horror stories that go with the infamous first year. Probably the only advice I ever received was the summer before I began law school while still working at the country club. A lawyer there, Richard, told me that law school was all about "PEP." Preparation. Endurance. Perseverance. Another lawyer there, Tom, told me that he and his pals had a running joke that no matter how hard it got, the law school would have to drag them out before they ever quit. I often went back to those two pieces of advice over my three years and either sighed or chuckled. They were on to something.

My orientation class didn't get the famous "Look to your left, look to your right, only two of you are going to make it" speech, but people alluded to it all the time as if to sort of water down the possibility of failing out. I heard many subtle nuances, but it was always the same overall idea: you will fail out, lead a sad, miserable life, and if you are lucky enough to get into law school by not lying or cheating, you won't be thrown out, but you'll fail the bar and surely become addicted to drugs while you are struggling with mental health issues. It was a common theme from day one, and it didn't stop until the day I was sworn in to the bar. Even then, I attended a mandatory continuing education class where the theme was repeated: there are no excuses, there are no do-overs, you will commit malpractice and die alone.

It was my dream to be a lawyer, so those presentations never made me question whether I wanted to join the profession. I told myself to just be me and that I would be fine. I remained committed to finding my way and making a name for myself, while constantly trying to overcome the fear I felt inside.

Law school is competitive, grueling, and rigorous, and it's not as glamorous as the Grisham novels make it out to be. It feels more like a meat grinder. I read so much during the first semester of law school that I went to the eye doctor for fear my eyes were going to fail me. My primary doctor at the university told me that he came from a family of lawyers. So much so that he was labeled as a black sheep for becoming a doctor. He once admitted to me that he could not have made it through law school because he never could have read all that was required. My existence became one of studying, persevering, and surviving, mostly through student loans. For years, I deferred a lot of future financial plans while living on turkey sandwiches, cheap coffee, and my dreams.

I felt like an outcast in the legal environment, especially during my first year. It was as if my 1997 Ford Taurus car screamed: *I came from the farm!* I quickly learned that nearly 99 percent of my classmates came from families of lawyers or other professionals. Most of them weren't first generation lawyers, and I had no idea. During my first year, one of my classmates said, "Oh, you're one of those." He meant that I was one of the five or so people in the class who didn't come from lawyer parents, but he made it sound like I was a leper. As I watched the amount of my student loans climb, on top of the stressful world I lived in, I became even more tightly wound. Through it all, I worked tirelessly to compete and do well, and I ended up doing *very* well. But the rigors I felt in law school were just the beginning.

* * *

If becoming a lawyer is hard, working as a lawyer is even harder. The intensity of a life in the law is ever present, and it is precisely the reason why older practitioners start harping on you about work-life balance, drugs, alcohol, exercise, and everything in between, on day one. I ignored most of the lectures because I never believed that I would become a drug addict or alcoholic, and I loved being a workaholic to get ahead. I told myself I flourished in stressful environments, and, on the surface, I did.

The day after I graduated from law school in May, we moved to Bismarck, North Dakota. As Sean and I progressed in our earlier dating lives, we felt the powerful incentive to live near our families. We agreed that Bismarck would be the city to suit us best. It was right smack dab in the middle of the long west to east interstate that we often traveled between our homes and college. And its population was growing toward one hundred thousand people, which we appreciated. We quickly settled into our rental space, and I began my self-study regimen for the late-July bar exam.

I started my job at a small law firm in Bismarck on July 31, 2009, just two days after I sat for the bar. During the endless studying that summer, I saw one bright spot when I met my friend and future law partner, Micheal. Because his name is uniquely spelled, I assumed I'd always write it incorrectly, so I immediately took to calling him Mike. While he was in college, he worked as a law clerk at the firm I was joining. Our first introduction was over lunch. My eating habits were so odd to him that he later admitted he believed there was something wrong with me. He too had grown up on a farm in the middle of two brothers, and he explained mealtime there as survival of the fittest. As he watched me eat very slowly and carefully, barely getting to my sandwich between all of my stories, he thought I was weird. Maybe our lunch connection was fortuitous, but we immediately became close friends. We also quickly realized that we struck a great balance together. He was impeccably pressed and oriented to detail. I was the charismatic leader and firecracker personality. We made sense together.

Three years later, upon Mike's return to Bismarck as a law school grad, we began to think seriously about owning a law firm together. The pieces all seemed to fit. We weren't yet thirty, but we had similar and proven work ethics. We were passionately committed to our clients, reputations, and the cause. Mike sat on a board for a homeless shelter, and I became the youngest vice chairwoman of a state Democratic party in the nation. My life in the law always seemed better when Mike was around because I was happier and more confident when he was there to help troubleshoot cases. He reciprocated the sentiments when he planted his roots in Bismarck to work with me. We had a solid foundation as friends and confidants and weren't distracted by a romantic relationship. Everything seemed well-suited for a successful partnership.

I knew it was meant to be, but I was hesitant. Owning a business wasn't anything I had ever envisioned, nor dreamed of. It also came with heavy responsibilities for me. I had my first baby just as Mike returned to Bismarck. And, by the time we became more serious about our own law firm, I had a toddler and a newborn at home, with a stay-at-home husband. Self-employment meant funding my own paychecks and health insurance, on top of my already piling demands at work and home. And it meant being the boss of others, which translates into headaches. Yet I believed that together we could be successful lawyers and business owners. I also desired to reap large financial rewards from my hard work and believed that self-employment coupled with my drive would make that happen. So I took the plunge. I left the familiarity of the only real job I had ever held and started anew.

Our journey together began at that first lunch, and as life went on we shared many lunches together. Literally. Mike ordered the French dip, and I ordered the Reuben. And then we shared. But I never ate any faster, and he still thought I was weird.

* * *

On June 1, 2015, at the ages of thirty-one and twenty-eight, Mike and I boldly started the Stebbins Mulloy Law Firm. We worked for two weeks at Mike's house to be a kitchen table startup law firm. After the brief period of endless meetings, calls, delegating duties to our new staff, and me finding time to pump breastmilk in the bathroom, we had a fully operational law firm. Stebbins Mulloy was an instant dream come true. Mike and I tried cases together, confided in each other, and made decisions together. We were the team we knew we could be.

It was busy and my days were a blur, but life felt good, especially at first. I really hit the ground running. I began taking in and taking on everything I could to build my future, including cases, committees, and an appointment to the State Bar's Ethics Committee. I was my own boss and made my own rules. And I seriously upped the ante. I set big goals. I wanted the business to make a million dollars, stat. I desired to be even more sought after than I was before. I wanted to quickly dig out of the financial hole that had covered me for most of my life. It was all right there. I just needed to make it happen for myself.

I became the lawyer I had dreamed of becoming since fifth grade, and more. I loved owning my own law firm and the empowerment of the senior partner status. I was nationally recognized for my success under the age of forty by Super Lawyers, the National Trial Lawyers, and local newspapers and was told that I was a force to be reckoned with. I enjoyed it all immensely.

I don't regret my decisions to tirelessly follow my dreams and to venture into business. But I believe that at the moment we swung open the doors to the new law firm, I cranked up my life to full steam ahead, and, unfortunately, I was never able to bring it back to a practical speed.

I was still too hard on myself. And I continued to ignore the warning signs.

PART II – THE ONSET

I'm out of control and out of my hands
I'm tearin' like a demon through no man's land
Tryin' to get a grip on my life again
Nothing hits harder than a runaway train.

"Runaway Train" by Elton John

CHAPTER 5

In early November 2017, I got ready for a vacation. I was taking my second-annual east coast trip with Mom for a few days, and God, did I need it. The year 2017 was raging in a way unlike any other. Life as a lawyer/mother began to feel impossible.

It all started in late-January when our family had just moved to a new house, our "forever home." We purchased a five-bedroom, two-story house in a desired neighborhood filled with green lawns, mature cottonwood trees, and beautiful, large homes. We loved the idea of sitting on the white, front porch with coffee, to watch the neighbors tinker in their yards and kids ride bikes. We desired three garages for the bicycles, wagons, and basketballs we were accumulating and a large yard for baseball, water fights, and a swing set. As we closed on that house on a Monday, after moving all weekend, I sat pale-faced and sweating and tested positive for influenza the next day. I had to lay on the couch for a week to recover, but on Saturday received a call informing me that an ice jam on the roof of our office building broke and flooded my office. As I gingerly walked up the stairs, Mike met me at the front door to prepare me for the disastrous sight. My space was the only one in the building to be affected, much less destroyed and left smelling like a swimming pool.

Given my nature to be run down and spread thin, if a cold virus was within a mile of me, I caught it, and it morphed into a sinus infection. I had never battled repeated sinus infections like I did through that cold and flu season. I steadily ate antibiotics from late-2016 through April 2017, which terrorized my already upset GI tract. I had been dealing with persistent diarrhea since it hit me walking out of a courtroom on an afternoon in August 2016, and no matter how many probiotics I ingested, it never left me. I tried to ignore it and attributed it to stress until a colonoscopy in June 2017, when I was diagnosed with lymphocytic colitis.

While I was provided some short-term relief from two light rounds of steroids, I kept looking for better answers. In October, my provider mostly shrugged me off and told me to attempt to control my symptoms by using Pepto Bismol. Through tears I said, "I don't need this." A chronic diarrhea condition wasn't something that was desirable, nor was it helpful to the life I led.

The depositions, mediations, and trials were incessant. I tried more cases in 2017 than I had in the preceding five years. I prepared, grinded, aggressed, tried to wind down, and then cranked back up in what became a repetitive motion for months on end. That fall, the entire burden of my schedule fell on me because my beloved legal assistant abruptly moved out of state, and Erica, our most trusted office manager and senior legal assistant, went on maternity leave. I was drowning in cases, and we were seriously understaffed. Mike and I both tried to grin and bear it, as we were happy for our friends, but it was challenging.

I was unsure and uneasy about going on vacation and started to feel anxious and nervous about leaving my children. I tried to bury the thoughts because I knew that I needed it. I convinced myself that a break would help me, even though my life and the office felt like chaos, and I didn't have a legal assistant to help during my absence. The anxiety and nerves prior to traveling were strange for me, especially my fear of leaving the kids at home since I knew they would be okay with Sean. I was excited though, as the trip we had taken in 2016 was one of the best of my life. I believed that once I got there, I would have fun. And I assumed the feelings were all normal because I was "stressed out."

But my stress was no longer acceptable and wasn't healthy. I was immersed in chronic stress. The kind that's harmful. I no longer led "A day in the life of a trial lawyer," like the videos I learned about in Torts class. A video like that would portray a busy attorney with endless phone calls, voluminous unchecked emails, an emergency hearing with a judge, a quick visit to the jail, and the other side dropping a box full of paperwork on her at 4:59 p.m. It would show periodic trials, a paperwork avalanche, and the juggling of scared and emotional clients with angry opposing counsel and crabby judges. But with proper balance, she would get through the days with time for breath, relaxation periods, routine vacations, and a time each day to shut down the noise around her and go home. She would see through a clear lens because the gravity of her job demanded it. A day in the life of *her* required enormous brainpower. She would know when to turn it off and unwind.

She would know not to burn out.

I had become a self-fulfilling prophecy. There was more work to be done, more victories to notch. I could always bill someone. I must work more. My desire was insatiable. To be formidable, I must continue to compete on this level. The goals I've set, I've achieved. Set more. Make them higher. Breaks are for whiners.

The stressors, predominantly clients, but also running a business, came and went in varying degrees, but I never let the stress leave my body. I couldn't go on a long and hard run. I hadn't been to yoga since the birth of my first child. It was rare that I stopped at my desk to close my eyes and just breathe. There was nothing telling my heart and the veins in my body that it wasn't always fight or flight. I sold it to my brain by turning it into entertainment. It became a big joke to people that my job was making my blood pressure high. I always said it while laughing.

My father underwent quadruple bypass during spring break of my second year of law school in 2008. His cardiac surgeon in Bismarck recognized his last name, having just performed the same surgery on two of his cousins. "Stebbins" meant heart disease, so my jokes weren't funny. I was compensating because I had quit caring about heart health and eating Cheerios years before. It was out of sight and out of mind. I was driving forward in my career, and my body had to be along for the ride. I gave it neither credit nor peace.

My emotions were dulled. It was too much to invest in the day to day of the sheer hell my clients were going through. It wasn't personal to me; I was only the medium. And I had never explored vicarious trauma. It was easier to stay at one steady speed, which for me became always frustrated, taxed, overwhelmed, and close to rage. I pretended that my emotions were separate from my body... my tired, sore body.

Too stubborn to ever stop and be mindful during the time, I can only define my burnout with the benefit of hindsight. I was an emotionally and physically taxed hamster on a wheel. I could no longer explain why I burned the candle at both ends, found holidays to be nuisances, and worked weekends. I could only justify. Outwardly, I said I loved my life, but I knew I hated my life. I was tired of juggling all the balls in the air of lawyer, mom, boss, volunteer, woman, spirit, body. I wanted more in my reserves for motherhood. Too many hours a day, my career got my full attention. There wasn't enough left for my second shift. I wondered if I still had close friends in my circle, since I had completely vanished from any social life, outside of a few drinks with Mike or a political gathering where I wrote a check and ate a few appetizers. Dates for Sean and I were a rarity. My routine 5:00 a.m. swims weren't enjoyable exercise; they were demanding. I willed myself into the cold pool. The dark circles under my eyes no longer hid under makeup. I was trapped under the weight of it all.

I continued to convince myself that with a little more time, life would get better. I repeated that the hours and busyness were temporary. *I swear I'll catch up, and then I'll strike the balance. Sean's with me, and we'll reap the rewards that lie ahead.* And I absolutely believed it.

Beginning in 2016, Sean and I began making serious financial commitments in our life. I kept repeating, "I don't see anything changing for me." All I saw were my professional capabilities and ability to generate income. I never once offered the caveat of *unless I get sick.*

Mom once warned me about working so hard and told me something might happen. I was incredulous, and replied, "Like what?" She knew what. She feared for my mental health. She had witnessed a major depression episode—her own.

In 1994, when I was a fourth grader worrying that I couldn't fall asleep, Mom actually wasn't sleeping. For a few weeks, she felt the severe and debilitating effects of a loss of interest in life, hopelessness, insomnia, no appetite, and lethargy. She sought out medication, and except for a brief time, never again went off it. With medication and support, she felt the symptoms lessen over the course of a few months. But she never forgot her onset and ensuing struggle. I don't remember seeing a change in Mom's health, nor do I ever remember her being away from her job. I don't have a recollection of the balance in our home being upended. Either I was too young to notice or understand, or if I felt the effects, they weren't committed to memory.

I can't really remember when I learned the details of her diagnosis. I feel like I've always known because she is remarkably open about it, and I've often seen others look to her for guidance through their own struggles. I've also seen her write letters to parents whose children were in jail, addicts, alcoholics, or died by suicide. I believe her openness about mental health is a rarity and a sign of her strength. But it was a characteristic that I had no intention of sharing. I could understand depression through her and what I saw as a family law and criminal defense attorney, where addiction and mental health issues were common for expert witnesses to debate at trial. But that was never me. It was never going to be me. I believed I would will it away.

I don't even remember the conversation where Mom warned me to slow down, and eventually she mostly gave up trying. Sean was no longer convinced that our deal was best for anyone—him always at home with crying toddlers and me always at work. But he didn't nag. He accepted our lifestyle and hoped it would get better with time. Mike also cautioned me about setting goals for myself and the firm. One time he even threw in a joke that in my wild pursuit I might do something to myself again like injure my legs. But by the fall of 2017 there wasn't much else for anyone to say. And if anyone brought it up, I became defensive. I continued to play back my narrative that began when I over-trained in high school, but with more intensity. *No one understands what it takes. No one understands what it's like to be me. Stress and breaks are for other people. I'm balancing it all. Everything about me is successful and planned.*

But I couldn't stand it.

I was burned out. And deep down, I knew it.

* * *

On Monday, November 6, 2017, the morning after the daylight saving time change, I woke up at 4:00 a.m., as if someone had turned on a light switch in my head. It was really odd because I never woke up before my alarm. I usually woke up at 5:00 a.m. to either start working at home, get to work early, or to go swimming. I planned to swim at 5:00 a.m. that morning, so I was not happy to have awoken at 4:00 a.m., only to try to go back to sleep and get up again at 5:00 a.m. But I didn't think much of it. I swam, got to work, and got ready to leave for vacation the next day.

I'd like to say that our east coast trip was really nice, but it wasn't. Something was wrong with me. At the time, we blew it off and chalked it up to the stress I was under at work and missing my kids, but it was something more. I spent most of the trip feeling restless, had trouble sleeping, had strange bouts of anxiety, and we ended up flying back a day early because I felt uneasy. It was all minor enough at the time, but it was there.

We spent the first night in Philadelphia, and it was hard for me to go to sleep because I was anxious. I believed it was because I hadn't ever been there before and that I would be better in New York City where we had traveled the year before. I convinced myself that I would be better able to maneuver there. I believed it to be more familiar and safer territory, which is odd in and of itself. The unease ate at me, and I didn't sleep well. I just needed to get out of Philadelphia.

Once we got to New York City, I wasn't any better. The prior year, I had easily led us around via the subway and our endless walking, but this time I became alarmed in the large crowds. A few times when the sidewalks were so packed, I held Mom's hand so we wouldn't get separated. When we walked on the Brooklyn Bridge, I felt like I was going to have a panic attack, which I'd never experienced. Mom was walking along enjoying herself, and I kept trying to pull her toward me so we didn't get separated by the droves of people walking with us and against us. She repeatedly stopped to take pictures of me and the view, which made me nervous. A man on a bike yelled at her as he nearly hit her, and it rattled me. I looked down at the steady traffic below me only once and was overcome with fear. I adamantly told her that we had to get off the bridge. I couldn't take it anymore.

I was constantly worried about us getting separated, or that Mom was going to get run over. It was as if everything she did in the city made me feel like she was in danger, and it overwhelmed me. Mom believed that I was acting unnecessarily scared and anxious, especially on the bridge. It was so unlike me that the whole event really stuck with her.

When we got to Boston, my anxiety mounted, and I struggled to read the map. Mom noticed it but chalked it up to my being preoccupied. She laughed and said she couldn't work a map any better, so she continued to follow my lead. I constantly stopped to look at the map on my phone and cursed it. I kept walking us around our mark and finally got frustrated. On our final night, I couldn't decide what to eat to the point that it was odd to Mom, and then I just wanted to go home. We changed our flights later that night and left early the next morning.

Unfortunately, the vacation wasn't very relaxing and carefree. I mentioned to a few people that it was almost as if I didn't have a lot of fun. I couldn't quite put my finger on it, but the trip just didn't seem to sit well with me. Yet, I didn't take much time to ponder it because I had to get right back to work. I moved on and acted as if nothing had happened. And so did Mom.

* * *

The anxiety had officially arrived, but it had been hinted at for a while. For a few years, everyone in my path tried to medicate me. When I saw Anne, a physician's assistant at my OB/GYN clinic in 2015, she mentioned vacations and medication. In January 2017, when I was struggling with sinus infections, I called my friend Carla to ask a simple question about antibiotics, but when I heard myself explain my life, it made me cry. Carla kindly referred me to a primary doctor, which I needed, named Dr. Joy Froelich, and I was thankful. Dr. Froelich worked with me to diagnose my GI issues, and we discussed anxiety medication. After my colonoscopy, a nice nurse who recognized me through mutual friends not only took wonderful care of me, but twice recommended that I begin anxiety medication. She even wrote a drug name on a piece of paper for me to take with when I left recovery. I appreciated everyone's input, but I didn't ever believe that I needed medication. I was averse to it. I just needed my work life to slow down.

I wanted the year 2017 to start looking up, and soon. December then became the grand finale in what felt like the year from hell. One day, as I sat looking at my calendar, raggedly fighting through colitis, the stomach flu, and endless court appearances, Mike came into my office. I told him, "I don't think I can make it through the month."

He kindly said, "You can do it. You'll pull through, just like you always do." But I doubted him.

I managed to make it through and had successful results in my cases and my year-end numbers. I hit my personal goals, and the firm grossed over one million dollars. I was elated, and the year was behind me. I fully intended to have a better schedule in 2018 because I knew I could never endure another year like 2017. I finally put all my goals behind me and hoped to live better. I was going to slow down and enjoy life more. It was time. And it was time for a holiday break.

A few nights prior to New Year's Eve, Sean and I went to a Christmas party and then a late movie. Movies were a rarity for us, but I wanted to see the new *Star Wars*. I felt unprecedentedly nervous the entire evening. In the theater, a man sitting behind me, but just in my peripheral vision, repeatedly got up and moved about, which made me anxious. The anxiety mounted, and I could hardly sit through the movie because I feared something bad was going to happen to me. I felt alarmed that I wasn't home with my kids and believed something bad was going to happen to them too. The movie itself even felt scary with the darkness of the galaxy and booming sound effects.

When we walked out after midnight, I told Sean I couldn't go to movies anymore. I believed I had anxiety because of the gunman at the *Batman* movie in Colorado, so I didn't want to go to a theater again. As we got into our frigid car, I realized that my thoughts felt very strange and seemed like overkill. But I was only convinced that I didn't like going to movies anymore, not that it was anything else. And I instructed Sean to drive fast and get us home so I could see the kids sleeping.

I didn't want to go out for New Year's Eve, so Sean and I stayed home by ourselves. It was time for a deep breath and the promise of a new year. We had a great time together watching TV and playing Nintendo, and the thoughts about the theater were a distant memory. As much as 2017 had tested me, a big part of me was proud of my accomplishments throughout the year. As we clanked our champagne glasses, I jokingly said, "Goodbye 2017, don't let the door hit you in the ass as you go!" I shouldn't have challenged the gods like that, but I did. I shouldn't have still felt invincible, but I did.

Months later, Ashley saw my numbers at the law firm and declared that my billables were inhumane for one person who was sickly, stressed out, and in a small firm. She was enraged at my work life, but it was far too late to tell me.

And I didn't know that my sentiments for a relaxed new year were hopeless. Something bad was going to happen to upend my life. It was already brewing inside of me.

CHAPTER 6

Against my hope, 2017 did not leave like a lamb, and 2018 came in roaring like a lion. January and February were continuations of the same pattern. I began burning the candle on both ends a little longer to catch up, but really needed extra sleep. Yet suddenly, it wasn't possible to come by.

As my kids got a little older and I felt less guilty shirking childcare duties for a few hours, I started taking long naps on weekend afternoons to catch up on rest, and to try to keep from getting sick. I easily slept for two to three hours at a time. But by January 2018, even though I was tired, I was unable to nap on the weekends. I also continued to suddenly wake up at 4:00 a.m. during the week, as if someone had set a daily alarm in my brain. The earlier wake-up time was very disruptive, and it quickly wore on me. It came with restlessness and anxiety that seemed to follow me throughout the day.

I couldn't make sense of why it was happening, so in late January I sought medical attention and hoped for an instant answer. I'm not sure what convinced me that the problem was my hormones, but I was convinced. I went to the OB/GYN clinic to see Anne. I told her about my chaotic life in 2017, but my specific complaint was my bizarre 4:00 a.m. wake-up calls.

Anne and I had a very serious conversation about my stress levels and how I needed a vacation. She also ordered blood work that day to look at my hormone levels and asked me to come back again in two months to repeat the lab work. I left hoping that I was on my way to a quick fix and remained stuck in my ways. I still didn't want to discuss mental health medication.

Tired and acting out on my frustration, I called Mom and angrily asked her why everyone in my path was always trying to medicate me with anxiety medication. She answered gingerly that day, but affirmatively; she told me it was probably because I needed it, and I could no longer blame my problems on the stress of my work. Mom's words pierced me. I started to give in to the notion that my work was having serious effects on my mental health. But I wasn't quite ready to talk to even Mom about the possibility of my having anxiety and depression.

I at least listened to Anne about the need for breaks and took action. Since Mike and I had opened the firm, I discussed taking off one day during the week like many of my professional friends did, and he always encouraged me to follow through on it. I decided to take Thursdays off.

One of the first days I took off was around my birthday in early February. I wanted to be near my computer because concert tickets opened up for Elton John's Farewell Yellow Brick Road final world tour. I bought Mom and I tickets to see him in November 2018 at Madison Square Garden, my dream venue for my favorite musician. I also bought Sean and I tickets to see him in Denver over my birthday, in February 2019.

A few weeks later, Sean and I agreed that it was time for a family vacation. We dearly hoped that an escape would reset my system and snap me out of my sleep problems. We believed that Arizona was just the place to recharge. We didn't tell anyone in our family, nor did we tell any friends, as we were afraid that people might want to join us. This was going to be a relaxed trip, just for me.

I had a vacation and concerts to look forward to, and I had a good new assistant at the firm. I was going to take Thursdays off and enjoy some extra time to myself. And I naively believed that a break in the land of the sun would reset me, and the sleep interruption would become a thing of the past.

* * *

In early March, we spent five days in Arizona. I slept a bit better, so that was good enough for me. But I had another situation where I had unnecessary anxiety, and this time it was at a spring training baseball game. The kids were tired and hot, so that alone made the game difficult. But what was terribly bothersome to me was the noise. Every sound at the game irritated and upset me. During warmups, it felt like the speakers playing pump-up music were blaring in my ears, even though they were far behind me. And during the game, when vendors walked by shouting, "Popcorn, get your popcorn!" I nearly jumped out of my seat. It kept scaring me, and I complained to Sean that they were yelling in my ears. After only a few innings, I left with the kids to stand near the entrance to the field. I couldn't handle everything around me.

Just like the Brooklyn Bridge incident with Mom, Sean and I legitimized it and blamed my stress. We even tried to laugh it off and said my job had made me a hermit. Also, just like the Brooklyn Bridge incident, I didn't think much of it, but my behavior really struck Sean as odd and a little over the top, even for me, who was known to exaggerate.

* * *

When we returned from Arizona in early March, I hoped I was rejuvenated and that I would feel better going forward. I also wanted to keep my nice Arizona tan, so I booked sessions at the tanning bed. On March 12, I went for my first session, and I accidentally burned my back. It was bad, and I quickly remembered why I had sworn myself off of tanning beds. When I went to bed that night, I tossed and turned and could not fall asleep. My back was throbbing, and I figured that was the problem. I got up and used an ice pack to relieve the pain, but nothing helped me get to sleep. I was awake almost the entire night and exhausted the next morning, but I blamed myself and the irritating burn. I quickly got moving because I had to leave again Friday morning for the State Democratic Convention.

The weekend of the convention was challenging for me. I didn't sleep much but blamed it on the hotel bed. I socialized and tried to have fun, but I was exhausted, and any alcohol wasn't enjoyable. I kept up a good face and enjoyed seeing old friends, but it was hard. I felt off, but only jokingly told a few people I had menopause. By Sunday morning, I couldn't stand myself, and Sean and I had a long drive back across the state to pick up our kids from my parents. By the time we got back to Bismarck later Sunday evening, I was so tired that I felt sick. I finally slept through the night, so I had some hope that if I got deep down tired enough, just like I felt when I was a little kid, my body would shut down.

The week after the Democratic convention was a whirlwind, and in the middle of it all, I finally purchased my "lawyer car." At some point in my life, I had decided that the mid-nineties BMW with a dark, metallic-purple paintjob was not going to happen, mostly because I felt like BMWs were for stuffy, old people. But something about the interlocking rings of an Audi screamed prestige and excitement. With Sean's encouragement, I found a new, white Audi I liked, but my dad, a true lover of vehicles, was hesitant about my buying a foreign car. Ever a practical dad, even as he was advising me in my thirties, he said, "It's going to be hard to fix." I politely smiled at him and purchased the Audi Crossover. The realization that I had attained something I had dreamed of for years felt monumental. The little car was sophisticated enough to drive me to the moon, but I mostly appreciated its great stereo system.

I also repeated my blood draw, and Anne let me know that my hormones all looked normal. I wasn't happy because I was still struggling to sleep and knew I had to look for other answers. When Anne and I discussed the results, she asked me about how I felt on vacation and again talked to me about the stress in my life. At that time, I was still averse to taking prescription medication and Anne knew it, so she suggested that I try an over-the-counter method first, like Benadryl or Melatonin. I agreed to those options as quick remedies because I felt behind at work after my trips out of town. And once again I had to quickly scale up my efforts because a trial loomed ahead the next Monday and Tuesday. I knew it would require a lot of preparation and performance from me, so I had to have all cylinders firing.

* * *

The weekend leading up to the trial was busy, and I was restless at night. As I drove to the office that Sunday, I called Mom and broke down in tears. I told her I couldn't sleep and that I felt like I was hanging on by a thread. Leading up to that call, neither one of us can remember how much I admitted about my disrupted sleep pattern, but I let it all out that day. Whatever I said struck Mom because she also told Dad about it and let me know that they would meet me Monday night for dinner. I was at least excited about that.

I worked late into Sunday night, didn't sleep much, and got up early Monday to finalize all my preparation for the trial, so I was already tired when I got on the road. But I had downloaded new music to take with me on the road trip in the new car, and that quickly livened me up.

A few of the songs I downloaded are now burned in my mind: "Let it Be," covered by John Denver; "The Boxer," covered by Mumford & Sons and Jerry Douglas; "Requiem for a Tower," by London Music Works; and "Hall of Fame," (featuring will.i.am) by The Script. At the time, they were just random songs I downloaded. They carried virtually no meaning for me. As the next month unfolded, the songs played like an eerie soundtrack for what was going on in my mind and brain.

I performed just as I always had in trial, but I felt like I was running on steam. Mom and Dad drove seventy-five miles to meet me for dinner that night. They knew I was struggling. As a little boost, Mom gave me a handwritten note with an inspirational saying and a matching Bible verse on it. I was thankful and happy to be with them while picking at a steak sandwich in an empty and dimly lit hotel bar because I felt uneasy about life.

After they left, I worked late in my hotel room to prepare for the next day of trial. I was so exhausted. I knew I'd sleep because I could barely stay awake. And just to make sure, I even took two Benadryl.

I fell asleep right away for only a few minutes and then lay there all night, tossing and turning between the digital clock that showed me each painful minute that I was not dreaming and the glare of the red light from the Burger King just outside my window. The songs I had listened to ran in my head to the point of madness.

I was incredulous at my body's unwillingness to nod off since I was exhausted, and I couldn't figure out for the life of me why the hell I couldn't. I desperately begged my body to please shut down during this trial. I pleaded for rest. I was scared and couldn't stand myself.

That night, in that hotel room, staring out the window at the red light, is truly one of the worst memories of my life. It is like my whole story and all the sickness set in on that precise night. My heavy chest and racing mind became a realization that something was wrong.

I barely slept a few hours and got up early to swim. I applauded myself for doing so well after such a bad night. I finished up the trial, pleased with my work, but worn from battle. I took off for Bismarck and was glad to have the experience in the rearview mirror, but I knew I couldn't go on the way I was going. As I drove away in my new car and blared the music as a distraction, my insides felt fraught. I knew I needed some help.

* * *

When I got home, I had no more hesitation about anything, including medication. I wanted to feel better, and I was starting to get desperate. I called Anne and bawled to her on the phone. I told her I couldn't do it anymore and that I needed an aid to sleep, something more than over-the-counter medication. Anne then prescribed Trazadone. When she told me it was actually an antidepressant, I was instantly alarmed. But I knew that I needed something, or my life was going to completely fizzle out. I began admitting that I probably was struggling with some anxiety or depression, and that was the reason for my insomnia. I hated to admit it, I hated to think of it, but I wanted some answers, and the answer of "lawyers are depressed" kept coming to my mind.

For a while, I only confided in Sean and Mom because I couldn't bear to see the tangling in my Superwoman cape. Recognizing my faults was one thing, but public admission was quite another. I eventually told Lacie when I met her for coffee on one of my Thursdays off. Lacie also lived in Bismarck and was well aware of how hard I worked. She agreed that I needed to start making time for me and was glad that I was at least taking a day off to start. Although, I ended up back at work for a while later that day. My staff noticed when I came into the office, but everyone knew better than to say much to me. My Thursdays off were short lived. I only did it a few times.

As Mom had heard the warning sirens going off around me for years, she always went back to her depression episode. She recalled how scary insomnia was for her and didn't doubt that I felt awful. She drew upon the similarities in our ages and having young kids on top of a stressful job, and it all made sense to her. Mom was thirty-six with three children at home when she was diagnosed. She strongly believed that depression was a logical conclusion for my situation.

I thought I was really happy in my life. I knew that I worked too hard and that the competing demands of work and home frustrated me, but I still recognized all the good surrounding me, and I still loved to laugh.

Depression. Use of the word alone left me feeling bad. I had dreamed of being Jackie the lawyer, and now I was Jackie, the *depressed* lawyer.

CHAPTER 7

By April, the nights had all begun to look and feel the same to me. To my right, the blue radio alarm clock with the large, green digital numbers that I had used since college. On the wall at the foot of the bed, our home security system box. The round button lit up in green meant Sean was still awake, and the home was safe. When the button was lit up in red, it meant that Sean was next to me, asleep, and it was late. The security system was armed, but I felt vulnerable. I would lie awake for hours, watching the digital numbers quickly move ahead and growing disturbed by the red light. The thoughts of the worst-case scenario pulsed through my head: *You've got to stop this. You've got to go to sleep. If you don't start sleeping, you're going to lose your job and your house and everything that matters.* I tried to convince myself that the scenario of my life falling apart was surely not going to happen and that I would eventually figure it all out. But the anxiousness and dread killed off my feeble attempts at reassurance.

I never tried to get up and out of bed because it seemed futile. I was too exhausted. Reading and television never crossed my mind. I just lay there and prayed through the terror in my mind. *God, please just let me nod off.*

When I woke up each morning, after a mere hour or two of sleep, I was crabby and upset. I vented to Sean and asked, "What the hell is wrong with me?" and "Why won't this shit stop?" I grew less pleasant by the day, and I knew it. It quickly becomes impossible to function without sleep.

I began sending early morning emails to the law firm to say that I would be in a little later because I hadn't slept well the night before. The short messages became a regular occurrence. No one responded with inquiries, and I didn't offer much more, just that I was having trouble sleeping. When I hit the glass door, with the etched Stebbins Mulloy and scales of justice, I put on my game face and hustled away another day. But I was irritable, and my patience was growing thin. I didn't worry too much about what the others around me thought because I was too preoccupied to care. Outside of being crabby, I didn't think I was letting on too much.

Apparently, I was. Mike noticed, and he started to worry.

Until the day I walked out the door for the last time, I had kept it together at work and was fully competent. I continued to balance all the competing demands, but it took all the strength that I could muster. My hindsight is that I was the equivalent of the functioning alcoholic. When everything in my life began to slip away from me, I clung to my work as the last resort. It was the thing I knew I couldn't lose, no matter what. I believe that my deep-seated conviction for my reputation and my drive to achieve were the things that gave me the strength to persevere for those months. And I didn't know it at the time, but I was checking things off at work, one by one, for what would be the last time of my career.

I had a trial in early April. I remember being a little tired, but the trial went smoothly, so it was mostly unremarkable to me that day. It's not unremarkable to me now. April 3, 2018 was the last day I tried a full trial. And it was in front of one of my favorite judges, Judge Sonna Anderson.

* * *

I started taking 25 mg of Trazadone on April 9, 2018, and it was amazing. For the first week I took it, I slept through most of the night. It was the miracle I had been looking for! As the Trazadone worked, my aversion to medication faded away. I decided that I could easily add a daily sleeping pill into my life.

On April 13, we went to a friend's for pizza, and we all had a few beers. I didn't sleep at all that night. I called Mom the next morning, and she told me that I shouldn't drink any alcohol with the medication.

I felt stupid that I hadn't even thought about it, but it was just another Jackie-type decision to act like throwing in a little medication was going to fix it all, and I wouldn't have to change much else.

After I talked to Mom, I also called a friend who was a counselor. I confided in her about my insomnia and my new medication. Knowing me as well as she did, she agreed that I was probably working too hard and that depression didn't seem out of the ordinary for the life I was orchestrating. We also talked about the relevance of my genetics with Mom's depression, and because depression and alcoholism were found on both sides of my family. It all seemed to make sense to me, and I felt better after speaking to a knowledgeable friend. I was moving toward acceptance of my mental health diagnosis.

The next week I slept pretty well and was still relieved that the medication was working. On Saturday, April 21, my family all got up early to go to Run 4 Change, a memorial run/walk. Our law firm was a sponsor, so most of the staff were there to participate. My parents were there too. I was tired that morning, as I didn't sleep much the night before, but hoped it was nothing. I participated by biking the 10k, and everyone had a nice day, including me.

The next morning, I went to church with my parents and the kids but was already exhausted. When we got there, the church was packed, and I realized it was a special event. I had to read during the church service, so I had to be there, and I knew it was going to run late. That upset me because I had work to finish. I didn't want to be stuck at church. I felt so smothered by anger and frustration that I went straight past irritability and flipped out, which startled Mom. When I left the church, I emailed the woman in charge and told her to remove my name from the list of volunteers. My plate was too full, and I could not donate any of my time. The dirt had slowly been piling on me for years and compounding over the past few months. But it was in that moment that I realized it and grabbed a tiny shovel to frantically pitch it away from me. I could barely breathe.

It all completely fell apart that night. I couldn't sleep. I tried upping my dose of Trazadone to 50 mg, but it didn't help. I instantly panicked. The insomnia was back, and the medication had stopped working.

I called my counselor friend again. If Trazadone wasn't going to be effective, I believed I needed professional help. She said something to me that day that embedded in my already volatile mind and stayed with me over the next month. She told me I couldn't just expect everything to change by taking medication and that I had to take more of a complete approach to help my problems. One of the things she mentioned that I needed to utilize was journaling. I understood that self-reflection and journaling were important parts of coping with mental illness, so I knew what she was talking about. I didn't immediately start to journal, but she definitely planted a seed with me that day. I believed I had to actively take back my mental health.

I made it to the YMCA to swim at 5:00 a.m. only a few more times. I often swam with my close friend Charlene, and at some point I confided in her about my problems. The last time I swam early, I told her that Trazadone wasn't helping, and I was in a frenzy about it. When Charlene and I replayed that conversation together many months later, Charlene vividly remembered that I was very upset and almost desperate. I was telling her that something was very wrong with me, and it worried her.

During the last week of April and into early May, I frequently called Mom to update her on how I felt. I called her a lot from the backyard, where I paced around on the phone while the kids played so I could talk and they wouldn't hear me. Much of the time it was in the mid-morning before I went to work. I distinctly remember asking her one day as I strolled outside, "Mom, do you *really* think this is depression?"

I told myself to just listen to my trusted friends and family and to shut up. I implored myself to just accept the conclusion that many around me were reaching. But I still had my doubts and couldn't shake them. From what I knew about depression, my situation just didn't quite make sense to me. I wasn't sad, and I hadn't lost interest in life or my job. I was just so tired. It still nagged at me, so I felt like I had to question it again.

During that conversation, Mom said, "Let's go back to what we know," which included her depression episode, how my situation was ripe for the diagnosis, and my heredity. In Mom's words, "Alcoholism is a relative of depression," and both could be found in my family tree, along with some anxiety. "Your great-grandmothers were nervous."

I stopped expressing any doubt after that pivotal conversation. I suffered from depression. I was anxious. Medication was probably necessary but would take some time and trial and error to be effective. Case closed.

CHAPTER 8

My longer than necessary morning ritual consisted of shutting myself away in my bathroom doing makeup and hair with a cup of coffee, while listening to NPR. That tradition continued on through April, just at a later time. I always wore my long hair down and loved dark eye makeup against my brown eyes. I dressed in my usual black or gray blazer with the alternating color of slacks. Although, in an effort to brighten up my wardrobe, I purchased a few new blazers, including a pink one that I began to wear. Everything about my exterior remained the same.

As an avid journaler, Mom began to document my struggles in her daily entries. On April 24, she wrote: "Jackie had a rough night last night. Insomnia is getting the best of her. She went to her doctor."[4]

When I saw Dr. Froelich that day, I admitted that I was struggling with depression and anxiety because of my workload. She prescribed Seroquel, an antidepressant, and I began taking it a few days later.

The next day Mom wrote: "Jackie is having trouble with insomnia, anxiety, scary stuff. I feel so bad for her–I've been there. She's cutting back on work, trying for less stress."

On the evening of April 26, I walked a few blocks from my office to the federal courthouse. I had been appointed to a committee by the presiding federal judge, whom I greatly admired, and we had our first meeting that evening. On my way there, I stopped at a convenience store to pur-

---

4   The quoted portions from Mom's journal are exact quotes, except for a few omissions which were minor and deemed irrelevant to the story.

chase Gatorade and chewing gum. I needed the drink for energy, and the gum was in an effort to keep from clenching my jaw. I had never before wrenched my jaw, so I figured the anxiety and insomnia were to blame.

We all gathered in the jury box for a welcoming and overview of the work ahead. As I sat there dressed lawyerly, with my briefcase, new spring purse, and Gatorade, I felt honored to have been appointed amongst the much older and more experienced colleagues. My spirit tried so hard to be happy, but my insides were writhing in indescribable pain. And I had a new medication to contend with too. I begged myself not to screw anything up just because I felt miserable, but I didn't want to be there. I repeated a mantra: *Just get through this, do not let the judge down.* I was able to make it through the meeting and head home.

The next day was Friday. I was casually dressed in a blazer and jeans when I called Mike into my office. I sat behind my enormous three-sided desk and felt ashamed. I was embarrassed about my situation. I was working too hard and everyone knew it, and I was upset to have to spill my guts to Mike after I had spent months trying to bury my problems as soon as I got to work. Through a lot of tears, I finally confided in him about everything. The heavy crying felt enough out of the ordinary, but what I really noticed was that my hands were shaking. I assumed it was because I was exhausted and emotional.

Mike patiently sat across from me and heard me out. We had sat in those same spots conversing many times, but this was different. We could read it in each other's eyes. He quickly told me that he knew something was wrong with me, and he was tempted to pull Mom aside at the Run 4 Change race the week before and tell her about it. He had decided to give me some more time to come to him before he would call her. He was worried about me.

I told him that I had to reduce my workload and that I needed more breaks. I planned to take a lot of time off over the summer to get well and reboot. I called it the "Summer of George," in reference to a Seinfeld episode. I believed that with more time out of the office, I would get better. He concurred.

We agreed that our jobs were stressful and that I had to stay on top of my health. Mike referenced his first week of law school, where he received similar lectures to the ones I received, about how many of the people sitting there were destined to end up depressed or abusing drugs. We talked about a lawyer friend of his who also couldn't sleep and was clenching his jaw. We agreed work and stress were to blame and that I needed to find a way back to better health. We had a very good discussion, and I felt much better after. I just couldn't get over how much my hands were shaking.

Before I left that day, I sent Mike the following email:

> Thanks for listening to me today. Sorry that it took me a while to chat—it's been a long and miserable process and I'm just kind of getting it all together (I hope).
>
> I'm very lucky to have you and I'm so fortunate for what we have at Stebbins Mulloy (even though it's killing us both slowly ;).
>
> I'll shoot the staff a little email this weekend to let them know about my Summer of George and then hopefully I can start getting back to normal.
>
> Thanks again.

Mike replied to me:

> No worries! Your health, well-being and your family are paramount—everything else comes after that. Please let me know if I can be of any help. I think you have a great plan in place and I'll be there to support you every step of the way.
>
> Can we call it the "Summer of Elton"? That sounds more fitting!

Nearly a year after we exchanged that email, and had that conversation, I saw the old message and was almost tortured by its simplicity. If Jackie can just have a little break, she will be fine.

On Saturday, April 28, Mom reported in her journal that she had talked to me and that I was "feeling better" on Serequol. I don't remember ever feeling "better," from the time I started on the medication until I left work. I think I just told Mom that so she wouldn't worry, and I was excited about going camping.

In an effort to defy the reality of how badly I really felt, and because we were fixated on the healing power of that summer, we decided to purchase a new camper for our family. I had deferred a large amount of earnings since we opened the business, and the number on the balance sheet gave me some freedom and peace of mind. We felt prompted to go shopping that weekend and found a beautiful brand new fifth wheel in the showroom. We were set to close on May 14, and everyone was thrilled, including me.

On Sunday, when I went into the office to prepare for the next week, I called Ashley, who lived two hundred miles away. At the recent Democratic Convention, I had told her a few of the details about my health, but mostly minimized it. I finally dropped everything on her. I wasn't emotional when I talked to her, but she was ready for what I said and offered an immediate and honest reply—"For years I've just been waiting for you to die."

I started laughing. But she was serious and kept going.

"I told [my husband] that someday I'm going to get a call that Jackie's dropped dead, and it won't surprise me." She, too, had been worried about me. She watched the way I was working from afar, and she knew it wasn't good for me. She was glad that I had sought out help and encouraged me to work with my providers on the medication to make sure I could get better.

We had a good discussion that day, which had gotten harder for us to do because we were both so busy with work, kids, and life. She made me laugh, and I knew I had her full support, so I was happy to have talked with her.

The next week, I took on a few new clients who had previously made appointments with me, but I turned away all other potential clients until the fall. Saying no to new clients wasn't something I often did, so it was hard for me initially, but I knew I needed to lighten my load. I assured myself that if I could endure two more busy weeks I would then leave the office for a few days and start to reboot. I also hoped that my medication would start working, but I knew it was going to take some time.

As I moved through the days, I kept trying to pump myself up and get myself going with my music, especially in the mornings. As I drove in my beautiful dream car, I continued to listen to the songs I downloaded prior to my March trial, but I became fixated on four songs.

I listened and sang the lyrics to "The Boxer" as if my life depended on it. "I am leaving, I am leaving, but the fighter still remains. Lie la lie, lie la la la la la la, lie lie lie." I told myself I was a fighter and that I could do it. I could overcome whatever was coming at me.

Two of the songs really pulled at my fraught insides. The first was "Let it Be," which I sang over and over, usually to the point of tears. A priest friend had told me long ago that when I felt scared I was to pray to the Holy Mother Mary, which I often did. The song began to feel like a prayer. As I was slowly unraveling, something in me was telling me to start trusting in God and to start letting go. A deep nagging said this wasn't going to easily go away, that it was out of my hands. So I sang a little louder, "And there will be no sadness, let it be."

I also listened to "Hall of Fame" on repeat, but not for myself. As my daughter and I sat in front of the TV one night after a bath, watching Disney cartoons while I combed her long, blond hair, a powerful commercial came on. That song was playing against clips of Disney princesses. It was total girl power, and it caught our eyes. From then on, she loved that commercial, and I appreciated the song.

When I listened to it, all I could think of was my little girl and what I wanted for her. Subconsciously, I was afraid for my children, who were only five and three. I kept trying to reassure myself that they would be all right, but I was scared.

I had a dark song too, "Requiem for a Tower." I listened to it one black, early morning, on my way to swim, and thought I was going to have a heart attack. It wasn't healthy in the state I was in, but I couldn't stop playing it. The song is as addicting as it is terrifying. It's deep, poignant, and powerful.

The chords had burned into my brain in college. At my older brother's recommendation, Mom and I watched the film "Requiem for a Dream" while I was on spring break. We viewed it in our living room at the farm on a bright afternoon, but it horrified me to watch. As the credits rolled, I just stared at Mom, too disturbed to even speak.

I would describe the plot as: Drug addicts sell their lives and souls to get high. Their physical and psychological states alter, and their dreams slowly die. Then they self-destruct. By the end, you barely see glimpses of the people they used to be. It's all painful to watch. And throughout, you're sucked in by the drama, but mostly by the orchestra music that plays throughout in a haunting and repetitive fashion.

The song was an earworm for the rest of my break, but I didn't hear it again until years later when I was listening to internet radio at work. When it began playing, it frightened me, but I loved it, and wanted it. The download of that chilling song was surely bad timing on my part, yet it was there to stay.

Along with my own music therapy, I heeded the advice from my counselor friend and began to journal. On Monday, April 30, I wrote that I wasn't sleeping very well. I described myself as: "very tired, dizzy, lethargic, irritable, anxiety, worry."

The next day, on May 1, I drove ninety miles to an out-of-town hearing. On the way home, I realized that I was too tired to drive safely. I felt alarmed passing semi-trailer trucks on the interstate and was scared that I would accidentally harm myself. I don't know if I said anything to Sean about it when I returned, but I knew I could no longer drive long distances until I got some sleep.

My songs kept playing in somewhat of an eerie soundtrack as my life began to unfold like a scary movie. I became an empty shell of my former self, while my physical and psychological states altered. I kept trying to pick myself up, but I was starting to fade away.

And through it all, a haunting song played on a loop. It was the requiem for me.

CHAPTER 9

The funny thing about a premonition is you don't know you're having one at the time. It doesn't have a feeling like deja vu. But by April, I had eerily begun living out premonitions and was silently saying *goodbye*.

On April 10, before heading into work late, I posed in front of our staircase. Under my blazer and big smile, I was showing off my new, gray T-shirt with the blue words "Foye Belle Foundation." I posted it on Facebook in solidarity with my high school classmate, Chelsea, who had created the foundation to aid cancer patients during their treatments. She was all too familiar with what a cancer fighter needed because she had advanced breast cancer that had metastasized. She was dying.

After exchanging Christmas cards, I messaged her on Facebook on March 31. Chelsea and I talked a lot about music in our conversations, and I kept encouraging her to listen to John Denver's "Let it Be." But mostly, we talked a lot about death. Chelsea had already accepted it and was remarkably at peace with her finite time. We were only thirty-four years old, so it seemed pretty heavy to be talking about death, but there we were.

I wanted to tell her that I was hurting too, but I didn't. I felt selfish even thinking about it. Cancer was spreading through her body, so that was no time for me to talk about being tired and nervous. She had already transitioned out of her successful marketing company. She was positive about the new owner, but it was bittersweet, and she hoped her legacy would live on. I believed that the conversations were the reality of Chelsea's situation and didn't have anything to do with me. I didn't question my own mortality, nor did I think of losing my law firm, because I was desperately focused only on trying to make it through my days.

On Thursday, May 3, I had to attend a short court hearing, as an ex-spouse had filed a motion for contempt against my client. Rarely did I ever attend court in less than a black suit, but that day I dressed more casually in a blue blazer and camel-colored slacks because the hearing felt like a nuisance. I just wanted it over with so I could get closer to my break.

Just as I reached the top of the landing, after climbing three flights of stairs, I ran into Judge Sonna Anderson. She was leaving a hearing and was still in her black robe. I stopped to talk to her and, from there, fate took over. It was one of the most candid discussions I had ever had with her, or any judge. I knew Judge Anderson only a little better than other judges, but on that day we talked like old friends. I knew that she had recently sustained injuries in a horse-riding accident, and you could see evidence of that for months because she had to wear an eye patch for her double vision. I had also recently found out from her brother that she had cancer. He told me that a lot of people didn't know, so I kept the news to myself.

We exchanged pleasantries, and then I just blurted out to her that she "looked so good." Her hair looked very nice, her makeup seemed bright and cheery, she had spring in her step and voice, and she didn't have the patch over her eye. We talked a little longer about life, and I again announced that she "looked so good." I felt weird saying it, but I couldn't stop. I was worried about her, so I hoped she was as healthy as she looked, and I wanted her to know I cared.

I wasn't excited to be in court that day, but something about Judge Anderson and me crossing paths just seemed to make everything a little better as I walked into Courtroom 303.

I performed just fine, and we won the hearing. Outside of my getting tongue-tied once, which may have just been me being hyper-sensitive about my state, I didn't notice anything out of the ordinary in my performance. But it was hard to mistake the blaring, white noise in my ears and that my right hand was uncontrollably shaking. When I picked up my water glass, my hand tremor was very obvious, and I hoped that my client didn't notice. I chalked it up to my lack of sleep and didn't worry much more about it. I kept up my mantra to just hang in there and that in a few days I would be able to leave work. I would even get to take my kids to the band parade we loved on Friday, May 11, if my two-day trial over May 10–11 settled.

That afternoon, Mike and I attended a quarterly meeting with our accountant, Ken. I always enjoyed our meetings with him. He was a valuable confidant and our most trusted business advisor. I also worked with Ken personally and began to grow under his financial tutelage. Business ownership had never been a part of my dream, but I felt like I flourished in the role of employer, and Ken assured me I was easily coached. I also loved the way he signed off on his emails, "See you at the top."

Many times after we met with him, Mike and I went out for drinks to debrief. Sometimes we had to process the decisions we faced, or the way Ken challenged us for growth. But more often than not, we were excited about the direction our company was going and how well we were doing, so we celebrated. That day was an exception. I felt like there was nothing to celebrate, and I wanted to leave for the entire duration of the meeting.

At the onset, I told Ken that I was depressed and was having trouble sleeping. I didn't cry in front of him, but tears welled up in my eyes as I had my elbows on the table and hands clasped in front of my face. I was still trying to mask the severity of the situation and felt no need to expand on my problems. I was also embarrassed to admit such a thing to Ken. He assured me that I was not the only person to have this diagnosis and that I was not the first business owner to suffer from the serious effects of stress. He seemed to understand my situation, and we quickly moved on to business.

As we proceeded to talk about the usual topics of our quarterly discussions, I felt like my head was in a vice. The ringing in my ears was deafening. The noise began to make life around me feel intolerable. And Ken was screaming at us. He brought up irrelevant things, only to yell at us. I just sat there and couldn't have cared less.

Mike drove us back to the office, and I could hardly even talk about anything, much less celebrate. As he was driving, he mentioned a few thoughts from the meeting. I remember him talking while I stared out the window as we crossed the railroad tracks, but I don't even know if I answered. I couldn't deal with decisions or heavy thoughts. I felt defeated and hopeless.

Ken wasn't screaming at us, because he would never do that. I also doubt that he was bringing up irrelevant things. It wasn't what he was saying or doing; it was all how my brain and mind were perceiving him and the situation. The meeting felt like an awful disaster, but it wasn't Ken, it was me. That meeting was one of the first times that I felt like I was going to crack and that I felt less able to respond to others.

I dragged myself back into the office and finished up some work. I braced myself for an out-of-town mediation on Monday and more of my committee work on Tuesday. I still had a two-day trial looming for that Thursday and Friday, but settlement was looking very possible, and I was hopeful for that. If I could make it through Monday and Tuesday, and my trial settled, I was home free.

But between preparing for the upcoming week and not sleeping, my weekend didn't go very well. Mom's journal reported that I had bad days, and I was not sleeping. Probably the only happy part of my weekend was on Saturday, May 5. I wrote Chelsea a message: "Hi dear. I hope you're feeling well on this Saturday!" As I wrote the afternoon message at home on my laptop, I felt like my life was nearly collapsing under me, and I was struggling to hold on. She replied that evening: "Hanging in there!! Loving you! Enjoy your Saturday!!"

After that, we never spoke again. Chelsea died on July 7, 2018.

And I never saw Judge Anderson another time. She died on March 10, 2019. The trip I made up the three flights of stairs to the courtroom for my May 3 hearing was the last of my career as a practicing attorney.

Whether it was fate or the random events of life, I'm so thankful that I had those final moments with those women, and one last victory in the courtroom. And just like Chelsea, the universe was going to take my career and business, and I would soon have the same bittersweet feelings about loss and my legacy. But I had no idea. Just as the premonitions didn't have a feeling, neither did fate.

CHAPTER 10

I finally said something scary to Sean. It's our best recollection that it was during the last few days that I was still at work.

I'm not good with an ironing board, so I steam my clothes in the morning to look presentable. As the steam flowed to combat the wrinkles in my pants, and Sean sat on our bed talking to me as I was late for work, I started to boil over. Exhausted from another sleepless night, I said, "I can see how someone could hurt themselves. After they haven't slept in so long." I just spit it out. Part of it was the way I handled stress, with angry venting. But it was so much more that day.

I used "themselves" and "they" as if to speak in the abstract. But Sean and I both knew it wasn't *they* I spoke of—it was me. I didn't want to hurt myself, but I was scared and worn out. My weariness finally lent an insight into self-harm.

Sean immediately replied, "You need to talk to a counselor." I mostly redirected him and assured him that I wasn't going to do anything harmful. I also agreed to make an appointment with a mental health provider. And then I desperately tried to get us both away from what I had blurted out.

Not only did that statement bother Sean, it frightened me. The daily struggle was winning, and I couldn't take it any longer. I knew that I was close to losing it without sleep or some help. I was afraid that I had even said it, fearing it would actually lead to self-harm. I didn't think it was a premonition or a threat, but because the thought had crept into my mind, that was enough to alarm me. I tried to convince myself that I spewed it in frustration, but I knew that my admission was out there.

* * *

I was able to be up early and ready by the time my assistant got to my house to pick me up for my out-of-town mediation on Monday, May 7. It was a beautiful day out, and the sun was shining. I wheeled out my briefcase and settled in for the hour-long drive. Mike and I had often traveled together for conferences or events, but having my assistant chauffeur me this time was unusual. I didn't feel safe behind the wheel. Yet, because I continued to look and act normal, my request didn't seem to alarm those around me. I sat in the passenger seat, drinking coffee and conversing along, but I felt anything but typical.

Upon our arrival, we quickly set up in an office and got to work. The mediator was one of my favorites and a close colleague, so I trusted that she could help us finalize the case. I came armed with the client's file, yellow legal pads, and facts. As I periodically dug in my briefcase for various documents, everything swirled around me. My mind hung with me, but my insides felt thin, like they were wearing away. The ringing in my ears and my shaking were getting worse. My body was becoming an empty shell.

I volleyed numbers and ideas back and forth with the other attorney through the mediator, and we settled the case by lunch time. Everyone was relieved, especially me. After we packed up and headed back to Bismarck, I smiled and repeated my mantra: *Hang on, you are almost done.* I held on to that little glimmer of hope in the form of a break as numbness completely overtook me.

The sun was still shining when I returned to my office. The phone calls with opposing counsel in the case set for trial that Thursday and Friday began immediately. We worked tirelessly via phone and email for the duration of the afternoon. By the close of business, we had a deal, and the trial was canceled. I felt like the weight of the world was off of my shoulders.

I also received a beautiful message from a client that afternoon. Through the years, I had received a variety of heartfelt thank-yous in various forms. I received flowers from a client who called me her "angel," and a dozen yellow roses from a good man in criminal court plagued by addiction, to signify that he sent them in "friendship." But the message I received on May 7 will forever stand out: "You are a rock star! Not only do I believe I hired the best attorney, but I've also made a friend, something I don't take lightly."

Just weeks prior, he had delivered a painting to my office that he made for me. He said he had painted it many times trying to get it just right, and I was the recipient of the final version. He explained that the photograph the painting was based upon was from the Great Depression. In it, a young girl sits on a small bench, next to a thin bed on a wooden frame, in a bare room. Her hands are holding her head up at her cheeks, and a bleak look occupies her face. Behind her left shoulder, some books sit stacked upon the wooden windowsill where a hint of sunlight lies behind it. He told me that if the little girl would just look up, she could see the light. She could find hope. She just had to look for it. The painting is a little dark in the literal and figurative sense, but its significance and the timing of its gifting are past irony or coincidence. It was a glimpse into my future. I was so moved and honored by his messages that came to me in my final days. It kept a little spring in my step that I so desperately needed.

That evening, I was able to fight through the feelings on the inside and put on a happy face. I attended a large gathering in an elementary gymnasium for my daughter's kindergarten admission meeting. I chatted with others, and my excited daughter and I took a picture together outside of the school.

I was also elated at the new mural in my home office, from my artistic cousin who painted the lyrics to Elton John's "Mona Lisas and Mad Hatters" on the wall behind my desk. That evening, I posted a photo of the lyrics on Facebook, and wrote:

> Some Mondays just feel like they take you by storm. When life is just so damn amazing and you're so thankful. When your ever talented relative paints your home office with some Elton lyrics to one of your favorite songs and you

love it so much, it nearly hurts your eyes (even if
you're wearing sunglasses). It was just that kind
of Monday!

The picture at the school became one of the last few taken of me. I still looked so happy, and full of life, holding my daughter's hand, with our big smiles and sunglasses. It took a few weeks for my physical appearance to start to catch up with the illness in my brain. And my excited Facebook post was my last on social media until I wished my dad a happy Father's Day on June 17.

* * *

While a senior in college, I went to the law school courtroom to watch the Eighth Circuit Court of Appeals hear oral arguments. I witnessed something fairly extraordinary that day but didn't fully grasp it then. As a lawyer stood arguing at a podium, facing a panel of black-robed, stoic, federal judges, he had a breakdown. I remember him stopping, apologizing to the judges, and muttering something about how he hadn't slept in a while. You could have heard a pin drop in the courtroom. He finally sat down, and co-counsel got up and took over the argument. I watched him sit at counsel table, slightly shaking, with his head in his hands for the rest of the argument. I just stared at him, and sympathy crawled out of my insides. It was awful to watch.

Stories of that lawyer's performance crept into conversation throughout my career. I usually weighed in that I was there and felt sorry for him. It finally fazed me as a practicing attorney how awful that must have been for him personally, and possibly his career. Yet I approached it with a more "shit happens" attitude than anything seriously reflective of what it would feel like to have a public meltdown as a respected attorney. So I'm very thankful that my nervous breakdown happened in the privacy of my office.

On Tuesday, May 8, 2018, I wrote the staff an email at 7:30 a.m. that said, "I'm going to rest up and take a bike ride. I'll be in just prior to my 1:00 p.m. meeting." I rode my bike that morning without any issue, except for being underdressed for the chilly weather.

I was quite late for my last day of work, as I didn't arrive until about noon. But I looked every bit the part of a successful woman in my grey, cropped slacks, a black blazer, a pink and grey shirt, and new lace-up oxfords.

I don't know exactly when the feeling began, but I started to dread walking up the stairs to my office suite on the second floor. I hated the look of the carpet on the stairs, and I despised the glass door I walked through where I had to manage a smile and a "good morning." Even the sight of my office made me sick. But the stairway was particularly potent that day. I walked each step slowly and deliberately. It felt like a death march.

Everyone was out for lunch, and I was the only one in the suite. I hung up my blazer, always preferring to work without feeling bound, and prepared for my committee meeting. I suddenly began to feel unease snaking through my being. I turned off the lights in my office and sat at my desk. I was short of breath, my chest hurt, I was scared and anxious, and I began a downward spiral. My mind went wild and blank all at the same time. I could not get myself to stand up, nor could I get myself to agree that I had to walk out of the door soon to get to my meeting. I was paralyzed with fear and could do virtually nothing. I knew it was bad.

I was able to call Sean. I placed him on speakerphone and laid my head on my desk to talk. There was no steam left in my body to move me. I felt very alone, and everything around me was eerie. I told Sean I didn't think I could make it to the meeting. I just wanted to go to the hospital. I could not keep going on like I was.

Sean had never before heard me sound so afraid. He sensed the deep-seated desperation in my voice. He convinced me that I would be fine, that I was almost done with work, and if I could just make it through the meeting, I could then go home and rest for a week. He assured me that my medicine was going to start working, and everything would be normal again soon.

He managed to encourage me, but he was actually scared to death. He was at home taking care of both kids, so he felt helpless about what he could do for me. He worried that he was going to get a call later that day that I had collapsed and was taken to the hospital.

His encouragement helped. I ended our call, picked my head up off my desk, and told myself I had to finish the job. *I can't stop yet.* I could not let down the judge who appointed me to the committee, and I had to see it through. So I packed my briefcase, donned my blazer, and walked to the courthouse for the final meeting.

Upon reflection, I'm shocked I was able to overcome my breakdown the way I did. I had a major panic attack. It was unrecognizable to me as my first one. And even though it scared me, my mind was already numbing. But in the depths of his being, Sean knew that it was bad. After our call, he tried to convince himself that I was fine. It would just take time for the medication to be effective.

* * *

The meeting ended in the mid-afternoon, and I fully participated. I was very pleased with the work of our committee. I was also very proud of myself, as I believed I added a lot of value to the group, and I had kept going, in spite of how awful I felt. But I was happiest because it was finally over.

I walked the two blocks back to the office, and while getting a drink I met up with Mike in our break room. We chatted about the day and my committee, and I told him very matter-of-factly that I felt awful. I said, "I just wanted you to pick me up and take me to the hospital." He was aware of my struggles, but I'm also one to tell dramatic stories, so I'm sure we both brushed it off because I also told him I was finally headed out for a break. He was happy for me, and we left it at that.

At 3:02 p.m., right before I left the office, I wrote the staff the following email.

> Everyone,
>
> Today was a long day so I'm going to head home. I'm super happy to say that right now [case] was filed and signed (trial is canceled); [confidential about the committee's work] and am done with that and I really don't have much on my calendar until next week. Thus, as promised, I believe I'm going to completely fall off the

face of the earth for about the next week. I'm still working on my meds and getting it all to where I'll feel 100% all day; I'm a ways from that right now.

Please just run everything through Jen and Mike; Jen can go to Mike and Erica with anything and I defer to all their minds. If anyone wants to know where I'm at; vacation! I set my out of office reply too.

Matt, just file [confidential] tomorrow by 5pm. Hopefully I won't need much else.

Thanks everyone. I'll be in touch.

I then packed a little bag to take home, which was common for me, even when I was taking time off. I had a yellow legal pad, a billing pad, my list of active cases, and the small blue planner I lived by. There were many future events on my electronic calendar, but I hadn't even gotten to writing down anything on my planner for the week ahead, which was odd for me. My to-do list and notes in the book ended on Friday, May 11. After I crossed out my trial that day, the only thing left was the excited note I had for the 6:00 p.m. band parade that Friday night.

When I got home shortly thereafter, I dropped my bag in my office. I stood miserably at the threshold and debated what I should do. I knew that I had an administrative hearing for a DUI case, and it was the next week. Something inside me told me I wasn't going to be able to handle the case, and it was a very strong feeling, so I listened. At 5:31 p.m., I emailed my colleague Lloyd and only wrote in the subject line of the email: "Will you please call my cell." Lloyd quickly called me back, and I asked him if he would take the DUI case for me. I told him it was brand new and that I thought I had some things coming up that would prevent me from representation. He was happy to take the case. I quickly arranged with my office to call my client and let her know that I couldn't represent her but that Lloyd was an excellent lawyer, and she would be in good hands.

That was my last official work as a practicing attorney at the Stebbins Mulloy Law Firm. From there, my emails go silent; my letters go silent; clients can no longer speak with me; my planner is blank, and I become a stranger to my own firm.

From that night on, the lights in my life start to go very dim. And so does my memory. For the next month, I almost cease to exist.

CHAPTER 11

I have only a few memories of my miserable existence from May 9– May 16. From May 16 until June 6, my slate is nearly blank. Some of the recollections are vivid, and some are distorted. Some are just lights, some are feelings. A few feel like memories but are actually dreams. All of this put together is like tiny emotional patches trying to hold together a large quilt of time and space. It's messy, and there's no beautiful pattern to be found.

I have only pieced together those twenty-nine days of my life through the memories of others. I wish I could view the month go by as if someone were making a video documentary of my life, but the footage doesn't exist. It's probably for the best because I believe the video would be too horrifying for me to ever watch. But I can read the journals I kept during that time, and that conjures up plenty of terror.

* * *

My home office sits just between the front door and the kitchen. Two lamps, a comfortable chair, and a custom desk suited for the needs of my bad shoulder comprise my workspace. I designed it to be relaxing and enjoyable, as well as an office; a place where I could read, listen to music, and work from home.

While seated at my desk, I face the painted Elton John lyrics. A bookcase looms behind me, filled with eclectic books, my music collection, and Elton John memorabilia. I loved being in my office. Yet after May 8, I immediately took up residence at only three places: a futon, the kitchen table, and the front porch.

Our kitchen table was highly trafficked by the kids, and it showed by the marks of crayons and old food stuck under the wooden chairs. My spot at the end of the table is where I journaled, just like my counselor friend told me about. I had already begun writing in a small maroon notebook before I left work. I jotted down a few things about "who I talked to," about my depression, and had some to-do lists for work around the house. I had also begun a timeline of my sleeplessness, appointments, and medication. I even created a playlist of songs that I wanted to send to Chelsea.

Once I left work, I started writing more in depth about my thoughts and feelings. My writing was a bit more ragged from my shaking, and I had already given up writing in cursive. I'm not sure whether or not it was a conscious decision, but considering I had exclusively used cursive writing over printing since third grade, it was a huge switch for me. I believe I gave it up as my shaking worsened. But I also think I realized that my brain wasn't allowing me to form the letters and connect them the way you do in a constant flow with cursive writing. I just couldn't do it.

My notebook, coupled with the smaller journal I kept in the psychiatric ward, are now powerful firsthand accounts of my brain deteriorating.[5] It's hard to have an exact timeline of all the entries because some things were clearly added to or inserted after the fact. But in the beginning, I think I was trying to create a timeline and was reflecting upon earlier days.

> May 6
>
> felt jumpy, kept startling awake
>
> -May 7-mediation OK
>
> -May 8-bad day ☹

---

5   All of my journal entries are exact quotes, except for a few minor omissions because it's irrelevant, not legible, or based upon the privacy of my children or confidentiality of my cases.

serious anxiety

May 8th-9th

Slept well, up a 4:45 am, less fatigue

Under "Positive self-talk," I legibly created and numbered columns named: Proud, Love, Scary, and Not Afraid. My pride and love were my family. Sean was "my rock [heart] would die without him"; "my kids [heart] I didn't think it was positive to love anything so much." I was proud of my achievements as a lawyer and success at a young age—"job, own a firm, good lawyer, competent lawyer & highly referred." Yet I questioned whether I really loved my job— "lawyer? Depends I guess–love/hate?!" What scared me was how bad I felt.

-don't feel like me, tired, fatigue, cloudy head, dizzy

-can't sleep! so fricking scary

-lose job

Under "Not Afraid," I pumped myself up.

-always bet on Jackie! she never lets you down.

-Work less!

-Work less!

-drink Diet Cherry 7-up.

I then created and numbered ten more columns, and I believe they were written on May 7: Talents; Contribute to my family; Afraid; Optimistic; Why this sucks; JMS 2.0; untitled; untitled; Thankful; and Adjectives. Under "Afraid," the premonitions were back.

-will this go away?

-when can I be JMS again?

-how long to be on meds?

-wore out my brain

-quit practice

-when will I sleep again?

Under "Optimistic," I boldly stated that I would "COME BACK FROM THIS BETTER!" And under "JMS 2.0":

-she comes back better than ever

-kinder, smarter, best parent & wife

-efficient

-Reduced stress load—don't do things you don't

want to do—don't make yourself

-more to do in life & community—more social

-work/life balance—fun—laughs

-need someone to love (kids and Sean); need something for work (I'm good at my job);

need some hope

Tucked between my optimism and Jackie 2.0, was "Why this sucks."

-I want to feel like me—like JMS—old me

-I want to be tired again

-I'm starving, I'm not starving

-I'm so dam tired I feel like death

-you feel like it will never end

-you wonder if you'll get out of it

-STUPID WORK STRESS!

The untitled seventh column comes from a book I frequently read to my children:

I think I can, I think I can, I think I can

I can do this—I will overcome this—I will beat

this.

I have all the HELP I need [heart].

The eighth section on the next page only contains entries and no title. I believe this page was written on the 7th or the 8th.

> You have to dig deep
>
> It takes all of your will power
>
> You cannot imagine the huge black
>
> cloud swallows you more & more by the
>
> whole.
>
> You feel like an empty body watching
>
> You feel too exhausted to do anything but
>
> move.
>
> You feel as solid as lead or light as a feather.
>
> Hail Mary, full of grace, the lord is with them
>
> Blessed is the among women & blessed is the
>
> fruit of thy
>
> Womb Jesus. Holy Mother.

The ninth section was entitled "Thankful," but it's a bit contrived when I'm thankful for my hair. And I'm writing as if I'm not the same person any more. "[F]unny–I loved being funny!"

I tried to describe my dark feelings in the next section, "Adjectives."

> -black, gray, rock, heavy, lead, weightless,
>
> scared, afraid, painful, worry, chest pain
>
> WANT TO GET BETTER!
>
> PLEASE GOD SEND ME HOPE!

I then reflected upon May 9-11:

> -got period Wed May 9
>
> -feeling tough May 10-11th, period, hormones,

-0 energy–0! fatigue

-black & creepy

-overwhelmed.

* * *

On Wednesday, May 9, I took my daughter to her preschool. I drove her in our van, and we made it there fine. But I had an eerie feeling as I accompanied her inside.

As I was walking through the door, my old legal assistant and friend, Chanda, was just leaving. Her child attended the same preschool, but I didn't see her there much because Sean usually handled the kids' transportation. When I walked by her, I still had my sunglasses on. As it looked like she was going to say hello to me and start a conversation, I grunted out a "hi" that was dismissive. It didn't even sound like me. And then, I just walked on. I remember Chanda's expression seemed surprised, but I just kept walking so I wouldn't have to face it.

What I remember about that encounter was not that I didn't want to speak to Chanda; it was like I knew that I couldn't talk to her, so I didn't. It was so uncharacteristic of me that it bothered me, but I couldn't help it. I was already in self-preservation mode.

I left the preschool and drove to the YMCA to swim. I had already stopped my 5:00 a.m. swims for a while because I couldn't get up that early. I got in the water and tried to do my usual routine wherein I would warm up for a few minutes, aqua jog for fifteen to twenty minutes, and then gently swim freestyle for another ten to fifteen minutes to finish. I aqua jogged for a while that day but stopped short of my usual amount of time because I was too tired. As I started to do some freestyle laps, I physically could not do them. I tried to do the front crawl for one lap but stopped while in the deep end. It was annoying, and I scolded myself to knock it off and just swim. I once more started to do the front crawl, but when I got to the shallow end I again had to stop. I stood there perplexed and angry until I finally just got out. I was tired and anxious, and I was mad. I had never before had to stop my workouts during my insomnia, so this felt strange.

When I got home after swimming, I reported to Sean on a few things. I told him that I no longer felt comfortable driving with the kids because I hadn't felt safe driving with my daughter that morning. I continued to believe that I was an unsafe driver because I was so tired. I also told him about how I couldn't swim laps and had to get out of the pool early.

Sean's concern began when I started on medication. When I desperately called him from my office, laying my head on my desk, he felt a knot forming in his stomach. My new reports didn't make him feel any better.

That afternoon, Mom and Dad came to the house as they were going through Bismarck and on to Fargo for one of Dad's appointments. I had already begun using a security blanket. It was an afghan my great-grandmother crocheted for me in 1994. It is magenta, teal, and yellow, just like the colors of Barney the Dinosaur. It was the only blanket I wanted to use when I would lie down or sit in my chair, and it stayed with me for the next few weeks.

As we sat together at the table, I started sobbing. I wore a long sleeve, white T-shirt, and a necklace I had strung together. I took a gold chain with an angel on it that was given to me as a gift for Confirmation, and I added a few other things on there like my great-grandmother's ring and a lucky penny from high school homecoming. I tried to bury my face in the neck of my shirt so my son wouldn't see me, but I was a mess. I could see the worry on my parents' faces.

"I want someone to just put me in the hospital, so I can sleep," I said.

"It doesn't really work that way," Mom answered with a sympathetic face. And I cried harder.

As I wiped my face with my sleeve, I said, "If Elton John himself came to my house today, I wouldn't care." My despair was met with silent nods and encouraging attempts at smiles that told me, *we care, but we are helpless to make you feel better right now.*

Mom recalled her depression episode and how it took a while for her medicine to take hold and get her back on track. She feared that the only thing that could help me was more time. In her journal that day, she wrote: "Stopped at Jackie's and visited. She started on Zoloft and

Ambien. She's taking time off cuz she's shut down."

The Serequol didn't affect me too much early on, but after I left work it messed me up. I reported in my journal that it gave me a hefty appetite for a few days, but that on May 8-9 I had "no appetite." I felt strange, and I also didn't feel like it was working, so I asked Dr. Froelich to prescribe me other medication. She chose Zoloft for me because Mom took it, and it helped her. I also begged her for some sleeping pills and hoped they would just knock me out. So she also prescribed Ambien, and I began taking the medications that night.

I tried to ride my bike the next day, but I had to quit. Just like in the pool, my legs wouldn't work, no matter how mad I got at them. So I gave up and sadly walked my bike home.

* * *

It was during these first few days off of work that I started what became my routine. I lay on the soft green futon in our living room, with my afghan, and looked at the china hutch, which had a tiny grandfather clock on it. I stared and listened to the clock's tick-tock. I didn't ever sleep. Even though I was lying down and tired, my body refused to rest. From May 9, 2018, until I landed in the hospital in late May, I didn't sleep at night, and I didn't sleep during the day. I felt like I was being tortured.

I was too tired to do anything else, except journal at the table and sit on the front porch in my lawn chair and stare. I didn't try to read. I also didn't listen to any music. I didn't watch any television or movies, nor did I go anywhere. My life was staring blankly and attempting to write.

I only remember using my phone to send two emails and make two phone calls. I did so as I sat cross-legged on the futon. Sean and I agreed that we shouldn't buy the new camper, so I first emailed the dealership and my bank. My messages were short but coherent. I then called two people to confide in them about my depression, and I think the calls were placed in rapid succession. I first called Rob, an old friend who lived in Chicago. I also called Betsy, a close friend from law school who was a practicing attorney in Bismarck.

Rob was very helpful and talked to me about his own struggles with depression and sleep. I remember crying a little, and we were both serious, which was very unusual for us. I cried quite a bit while talking to Betsy and rehashing the events of the past few months. What struck me the most from our call was when Betsy said, "Jackie, you're sick." Her words really hit me because I hadn't yet admitted to myself that depression was an illness. And mine felt severe.

For the few weeks prior to my leaving work, I often sat on the porch in the morning before I left, and I frequently saw our neighbor, Dorothy, outside tending her flowers. We had gotten to know Dorothy and her husband Roger fairly well, and I was very fond of them. On the mornings I would see her, we would both wave at each other.

A few days after I left work, I went outside and, just as I went to plop down in my chair, I saw Dorothy. I gave her the most dismissive, white-flag-type wave that I could muster. Just like my encounter with Chanda at the preschool, I wasn't mad at Dorothy, far from it; I just couldn't take it anymore. I had no social capital to give.

Sean came out a little later, and I angrily asked him, "Does she know?" Meaning, does Dorothy know that I'm depressed?

He quietly said, "Yes, she knows."

She had seen me sitting outside quite a bit and asked Sean about it, so he had confided in her that I was depressed. She was very supportive and talked with Sean about depression, which helped him. But it also gave him pause because much of what Dorothy told him that day didn't seem to relate to my situation. Another neighbor weighed in after she also noticed me hanging around the house a lot. She had a similar conversation with Sean, and her analysis also didn't seem to fit my symptoms. Sean hoped that I was just different and that my medicine wasn't yet effective. But the knot in his stomach again twisted.

On May 10, Mom wrote: "Jackie's having a rough time. I know the feeling and it's awful. I offered to stay with her. We came home." On May 11 she wrote: "I broke down and cried."

On our family's weekly white board in our entry, three events were written in black marker: Wednesday afternoon, Mom and Dad were visiting; Wednesday evening, Sean and I planned a date night; and Friday night, the band parade I hoped to take the kids to.

Friday evening, May 11, came and went, and I couldn't leave the house. I remember lying on the futon and sitting on the porch that afternoon, watching it mist and lightly rain outside. Sean didn't believe I felt well enough to go, and I didn't argue. It made me sad, but we missed the parade.

Friday night concluded the week's plans. It became the last of what was supposed to be a routine work week in our household. The whiteboard and its three entries stayed frozen in time and went unerased for months. And a week at our household was never again the same.

CHAPTER 12

Our bedroom has light-gray walls and soft lighting. As the sun fades in the evening, you can see the tops of our large cottonwood trees in the backyard through the windows, and you can hear them swaying in the wind. It's a very relaxing room. Unless your brain is sick.

Before I left work, I described myself as: "very tired, dizzy, lethargic, irritable, anxiety, worry, and jumpy." On May 9, after taking an Ambien, I journaled: "up at 3:30 a.m.," "felt confused and scared," "jolting awake with my whole body."

While taking Ambien, I was full of anxiety, strange behavior, and jittery questions. I was so restless that it was hard for Sean to sleep with me, and he was unnerved at my behavior. It's his opinion that my eyes were shut but that I was never asleep. He began sleeping in the kids' rooms so he could rest, but also so he was close enough to monitor me.

On the night of either May 10 or 11, I became terrified while in bed because I saw grey waves of dead people floating over me. I could feel them above me. I don't think I recognized anyone, but I knew they were dead. I was lying flat on my back with my arms out to my side, looking up. I've often heard of near-death experiences as the person floating above their body, seeing life go on under them, and seeing light or a bright tunnel. I saw none of that, but I was terrified. I yelled for Sean and asked him, "What's wrong? Where am I?" He tried to calm me down while I lay there almost paralyzed with fear, unable to explain the horror of the gray waves of death.

I also began sleepwalking and wandering in the house. Sean recalls that, at first, I stayed in my room. He heard me but assumed that I was getting up to go to the master bathroom, so it didn't alarm him right away. Shortly thereafter, I started to wander more, and he could hear my footsteps moving around upstairs. When he heard me walking around, he began to check on me.

One time, as he was walking up the dark stairs to check on me, he heard noises. He heard our bedroom door, right at the top of the staircase, making the noise of sweeping over the carpet, just as it does when the door opens or closes. *Shhhht. Shhhht. Shhhht.* When he realized that the door was repeatedly opening and closing, his heart began to race. He thought that either I was doing it or that someone else was in the house. He grabbed the door, held it, and said, "Honey?" to see if I was on the other side. Then he dashed through the door and turned on the lights. I just stood there, alarmed and confused.

He asked me what I was doing, and I replied, "I don't know." I then started asking, "What do I need to do?" He reassured me nothing, that I was in my bedroom and that I needed to go to sleep.

I then started bursting into the kids' rooms while he was sleeping with them and asking him, "What's going on?" or, "What do I need to do?" Sometimes I quietly walked into the kids' rooms and watched them. He was worried I would wake them up, so he'd gently guide me out of their rooms and back to mine. I was always very relieved when I saw the children, and I'd tell him they were okay, as if I believed they were not okay until I checked on them.

On May 11, I wrote:

in and out a lot, little less confused

so so so very very very tired

I am so tired!

After all the week's events, Sean asked me if I wanted to go to my parents' home in Bowman for the weekend, to give me a change of scenery and to be around family. I agreed that it would probably help. Sean also hoped for a little break from my scary and erratic nighttime behavior.

That same day, at 12:38 pm, a call to my phone went to voicemail. "Hi Jackie, it's Charlene. I just wanted to see how you're doing and to see what's going on. I just wanted to check in."

* * *

We left for Bowman on Saturday morning, May 12. I wore a sweat suit, and I took my afghan with me. I covered up with it and held it in the van during the whole trip there and back. I was mostly silent as we drove.

I don't remember much about being at Mom and Dad's that weekend, except that I felt so miserable I could hardly talk or eat, and I just lay on the couch. I stared a lot and kept saying, "I feel empty." It was apparent to everyone that I felt awful and was not myself. I remember my Grandma Ruth coming over to eat lunch with us and talking to me some. Sean vividly recalls the way she looked at me. He could see the fear in her eyes and on her face, and it nearly crushed him.

That day, Mom journaled: "Jackie thought she'd feel better here. She ate a little. So weak and trying to wrap her mind around this."

In my journal, I wrote:

-at Mom & dad's, van ride ok

jaw feels like it's tight, closed, clenched & chattering it makes NO sense.

That afternoon, Mom, Dad, and I got into Dad's black pickup and drove down the red gravel roads past the familiar neighboring farms. The weather was dreary, and there was a damp mist in the air. The scene outside entirely matched my psyche within: dark, cloudy, and cold.

I hadn't been back to our farm in almost exactly ten years, since my parents had sold it and moved into a home just outside of town. As Dad's health declined, my parents made the very difficult decision to sell the place and land that held family history and immeasurable value. I had spent my last night there on a cool August night in 2008, by myself, before I traveled back to Grand Forks to complete my final year of law school. I had never liked to stay at the farm alone, but I felt compelled to that night. Everything around me was very dark, except for the star-filled sky. It was unnervingly quiet there in the house, empty of everything but memories.

I believed myself to be at peace with the loss of my childhood home. Yet after that last night, I couldn't bring myself to visit. In 2014, when I first heard Miranda Lambert's song "The House that Built Me," I cried. I felt like she wrote that song for me.

My return to my childhood home a decade later carried profound meaning for me. We didn't go into the old place, as I didn't want to see anyone, but we stopped on the hill and looked down in the valley where the farmstead sits, and all around at the vast prairie lands. I felt nothing but exhaustion and despair, but the familiar sights gave me some peace. I was like an old dog who wanted to go home to die. Miranda's lyrics silently played in the background... *I thought if I could touch this place or feel it, this brokenness inside me might start healing.*

* * *

That night, I went to bed in one guest room, while Sean and the kids slept in the other room. In a panic, I started yelling for Sean very loudly. I kept asking him, "What's happening to me?" I also asked, "Am I dying?" Sean repeatedly assured me that I was at Mom's house, and I was okay, but I just lay there, flat on my back with my arms out to my side, and repeated, "What's happening to me?" I later barged into the room while he and the kids were asleep and asked him similar questions.

I was acting afraid, just like when I saw the dead people floating over me, but my behavior was even more intense this time around. Nights were bringing out the worst in me. Sean immediately wished that we were back at our home, where we had the security system to monitor me and any of my movements at night.

The next morning, May 13, was Mother's Day. Sean tried to give me a gift from him and the kids, which was a spa gift certificate, but I just lay there and stared and didn't really understand what it was. I was still messed up from the night before. I did take a photo with Mom that Mother's Day, and just like all the days leading up to it, I still looked entirely normal and just like myself. But there are no photos of me with my kids.

From taking my daughter to school on May 9, until the night of May 14, when I was checked into the psychiatric ward, I have no recollection of my children at all. I don't remember how I acted with them, how I encountered them, if they came to me for affection, what they wore, or what they did. *I remember nothing.* Not even when my daughter gave me a Mother's Day gift that she had made at preschool.

Sean assures me that, at the time, I continued to interact with the children, and they didn't notice too much of a difference in me, but the thought of my situation unfolding in front of them hurts me. It's an evil thing to take a mother's mind from her in the presence of her children. My rapid demise was in plain sight. They saw it all. They were witnesses to my mental and physical failure. Even with my lack of memory, it's devastating.

On Sunday, Mom journaled: "Jack and I and the kids went to church. Jackie can't go. We did sit outside and visit. She doesn't talk much just stares off in the distance. They went home about 4:00 p.m."

On the drive home, I only remember that I had my afghan on me, and Sean and I talked about how we would try to go to Bowman for all the weekends that it took, until I started feeling better. I agreed that was a good plan.

My journal entry from May 13 states:

-so very fatigued, can't walk stairs, can't shower

-I feel like death

-my chest hurts

-so tired—so shakey—so zoned

-head feels like a blender & a spinning top

It is only now, with hindsight, that I can say from about the time I left work, until early June, there was truly nothing on my mind. There were no thoughts, no music, no lyrics stuck in my head, no funny quotes from movies, no situations playing out, no memories, no current events, no news, no hopes for tomorrow, no excitement about any plans—there was absolutely nothing past staying alive. My only consciousness was of the sickness in my insides.

CHAPTER 13

I have no memory of returning to Bismarck on Sunday evening, May 13, or of us taking our daughter to preschool that Monday morning.

Early that day, I wrote a few entries:

Tired

-you are just so tired, but you cannot sleep

you keep thinking you will just nod off, but you don't

who could want to feel like this—why would someone

want to alter her mind

every day—you say—this is it—I'm better I'm

me now—can I ever even be me? And if

it led me to feeling like this—I must have

been something.

Sunshine

So nice on my warm body

So glad its finally summer too

Camping is the memory maker forever

I still had my legs & arms, still had those lungs,

then it

all just quit (5-11-18) can barely walk around

the block.

-played with [my son]

-fed [my son] cereal from breakfast

-SOME GLIMMER OF HOPE!

-PLease God—heal me—please make me be

me again

At some point that morning, Mike and I began texting about the firm, and our conversation got a little strained. I told Mike, "I can't come back."

Mike replied, "What do you mean you're not coming back?"

I said, "Something's wrong with me. I feel like I'm in a coma."

I remember thinking that Mike was not understanding how sick I was, even though I was trying to tell him. But in his defense, he hadn't seen me since I had left the office. He saw me again soon enough.

I saw that text thread many months later, when I dared to review some of the texts still on my phone. Reading the messages brought back the extreme fear I felt that day, my sense of Mike's reaction, and how I knew my life was in a tailspin. I then deleted it, hoping to never revisit it again. About a year later, when Mike and I met to discuss the transition of our law firm, he brought up our messages from that day. He relayed to me that he was on his way out of town for a hearing when I told him that I couldn't come back and that something was wrong with me. It was all very unnerving to him. Reliving that conversation much later was still upsetting for both of us.

* * *

Early that afternoon, Sean told me that Ashley had called him and that she was driving in from Fargo. She was going to take me to see her Aunt Melanie, a social worker, and then she was taking me to the hospital to check me into the psychiatric ward. When Sean told me that, I was so happy and so relieved. I muttered "thank-you." It felt like someone was finally going to get me some help and take me to the hospital, like I had been begging for.

My family had held off on admitting me because they believed the medicine needed time to take effect. We were also waiting for me to see a counselor. At about the time I left work, I made an appointment, but I couldn't get in until May 16. The weeks leading up to that appointment felt like they took forever, but we held hope that it would help. When Ashley called and said that she wanted to take me into the hospital, I was overjoyed because I didn't feel like I could wait any longer.

Although I don't remember, I was evidently still communicating with Ashley after I left work and had told her I desperately needed help. She didn't want to idly listen any longer and decided to act. Sean started crying when Ashley called him to say that she had heard enough and that someone had to do something for me. He knew I needed help and that it was time to get me some. He, too, was done waiting.

Sean told Ashley to talk to Mike and asked that she also bring in my trusted friend Betsy, so she did. He knew that appropriate measures would need to be taken at the law firm in my absence, but he couldn't help because he wasn't a licensed attorney. Ashley then talked to both Mike and Betsy, and they devised a plan to take care of my cases to make sure that none of my clients were affected while I was out for an extended medical leave. Considering that I had begged to be checked into the psychiatric ward, everyone knew that I wouldn't be back to practice for a while. Sean thought that everything sounded acceptable, and he approved of the plan.

I remember Sean telling me that Ashley directed me to write out a status memo about my active cases so she could meet with Mike and Betsy, and they could divide them. I didn't ask any questions, and I did exactly what she asked me to do. I sat down at my spot at the kitchen table with my list of active cases, my planner from the week before, and a legal pad, and I wrote out what the others would need to know. I didn't struggle to do it, and I don't remember having any problems writing down what needed to be done for each client and each case.

Ashley believed that subconsciously I was ready to pass on all my cases and was very organized for the final transfer. She believes I knew I was done. In my memory, I was at peace with letting clients go because I knew I wasn't equipped to competently handle cases. But she states that I was adamant not to have any cases and wanted them all off my plate.

* * *

In the early evening, I sat on my bed with my bag next to me, and I waited for Ashley to arrive. I was wearing grey, striped tights and a grey Dallas Cowboys T-shirt that Sean bought me at Cowboy stadium. I didn't have any makeup on, as I had not worn any since I left work, and my long hair was casually pulled up. I don't know what I packed or how I packed, but I did. I used my purple Speedo swimming bag that had my shower sandals and some toiletries in it, and I think I put a few clothes in there. Given the shape I was in, I'm not sure whether I was prepared to leave home. More importantly, I had never before packed myself for a stint in a psychiatric ward, so I didn't know that I wouldn't be allowed my things.

When I heard Ashley come in our front door, I immediately became very emotional. When she got upstairs and came through the doors to my room, I started sobbing uncontrollably and was shaking. I hugged her tightly and was apologetic. It was all strange behavior for me. She was very positive and told me that although it was a terrible situation, and she knew that I felt horrible, I was going to get better.

We made our way downstairs, and I sat in my recliner while Ashley and Sean talked. That day was the beginning of people conversing about me and making plans for me, without my knowledge or input because I was unable to participate. I was losing control over what was going on around me.

I don't remember who came in next, Mike or Betsy, and I don't remember either of them walking into the house. It's all an emotional blur. I only know that when one of them came in, or both of them, I turned and buried my face into my recliner to cry, like a little kid would do to hide herself. I was also trying very hard to not let my kids see me in the state I was in, but I couldn't control myself. I know that I was happy that Betsy was there, but I can't recall her appearing or my specific reaction to her.

I do remember a scene between Mike and me, and it elicits deep and strong feelings. I walked briskly to meet him in the middle of my living room and hugged him tightly around the neck. I envision my embrace the way a mother hugs a son who is headed off for war. While holding on to him, I cried uncontrollably and loudly repeated into his right ear, "I'm so sorry, I'm so sorry."

I knew that my absence was going to be greatly noticed at the law firm and that suddenly the weight of the business was going to be dumped upon Mike. And given the text messages we shared that morning, I knew Mike was scared too. Worse yet, by that day I had it set in my mind that I had done everything to myself. I had worked too hard, I had lost focus on life, I let go of any balance I ever had. I was obsessed with my business, and I let family law ruin me. I was very sick, and it was all my fault. That was all going through my head as I was squeezing Mike and apologizing to him.

Ashley and Sean quickly escorted me to the garage to get in the car while Mike and Betsy took care of the kids and distracted them with McDonald's for dinner. I can just barely picture them sitting at the table beside the kids, talking to them, and the kids looking happy as I walked out. I didn't hug the kids or say goodbye to them because I was too much of a mess. I was also devastated that I was leaving my kids to check into the psychiatric ward, even though I knew I needed it. It was about the darkest and worst feeling I had ever had as a mother.

The three of us got in the car and headed to Melanie's office. Overall, I think I knew it was truly the strangest time in my life, but I was okay with it because I was finally going to get the help I needed to be able to sleep again.

* * *

At about 6:00 p.m., on Monday, May 14, Ashley, Sean, and I arrived at Melanie's office, where she was waiting for us. Melanie is a well-respected social worker in North Dakota. As much time as I had spent around Ashley's family, I knew Melanie quite well and I thought the world of her. I was very happy that she wanted to help me.

A long time after this event, Ashley admitted to me that as she drove to Bismarck from Fargo, with the full intention of checking me into the psychiatric ward, she quickly realized that she wasn't exactly sure what she was supposed to do. Thus, she had called her Aunt Melanie, who said she would assist us. I had never questioned why Melanie was involved at the time or even after, as it had always made sense to me.

I was in no better shape by the time we got to Melanie's office. She met us at the door, hugged me, and I bawled all over her. We went into a small conference room and talked around a table. I sat across from Melanie, Sean sat next to me, and Ashley sat at the far end on my right side. Melanie proceeded to ask me some questions about my situation, my lack of sleep, and signs of mental illness, and I was able to answer.

What I remember most is how I completely lost it and blamed the status of my life on myself and the practice of law. And I finally shared a story I had tried to bury.

In May 2017, I took a quick trip to St. Paul, Minnesota, for a legal conference. I flew in early to meet one of my close friends from law school, Kadee, who lived and practiced there. We had a fun day together, and I spent a lot of time with her son. He was much older than the baby I had known in law school, and we really buddied up. Kadee had just gotten a divorce, and her son brought it up to me that day as we hung out.

We all went out to lunch together before Kadee dropped me off at my hotel. As Kadee and I swapped our lawyer stories, her son looked up at me and sincerely asked, "You don't do any law with kids, do you?"

My answer flew out of me. I could hear Kadee trying to speak up to answer him as well, and I knew she was going to tell him that it was my job. I cut her off and spoke over her to say, "No, I don't do anything that involves kids." And I ended it. I knew I lied, and I knew that Kadee was doing the right thing by trying to explain my work, but I didn't care. I decided that I could not look at his innocent face and know his struggles with divorced parents and admit to him that I was a part of that in other kids' lives. Kadee looked at me blankly as if to say, *Wow,*

Jackie, that's not true. But I ignored it and repeatedly told myself that I had done the right thing; I had protected him. Divorce was his harsh reality, but I didn't want to tell him that I was a part of that world. It was best to lie.

What I wouldn't admit to myself was the greater problem that I knew loomed ahead for me—explaining to *my* children what I did for a living. I feared it would subject them to bullying or ridicule, especially as my reputation as a family law pitbull grew. No matter what I told myself, I was ashamed about lying to Kadee's son, and I feared what I was going to tell my own kids. But I didn't ever try to address it again with Kadee or anyone else. I bottled it up. Until I got to Melanie's office.

As I shared the exchange in St. Paul, I became even more emotional. I admitted that my work and business dominated my life, and I felt like I had turned into a miserable, awful person. I believed that family law was at the root of all of my problems, and I said repeatedly, "I'm done, I'm done." And then I just gave up and sobbed.

Melanie asked me which hospital I preferred and then made some calls. I preferred St. Alexius/CHI Hospital, but after her calls Melanie believed it best for me to check into Sanford Hospital, which I was fine with. Whether it was fate or divine intervention that I ended up at Sanford, it was the best thing that happened because if not for my landing at Sanford, I would not have met Nurse Practitioner Stephanie Macdonald the next week, whom I credit with saving my life.

Melanie hugged me, assured me that I was going to get better, and we left for the Sanford Emergency Room.

* * *

I don't recall much from the ER, except sitting in a room with Ashley and Sean for a bit, and then being by myself for quite a while. I also remember the staff doing some blood work and telling me that they were trying to determine whether I had a medical or behavioral issue. I don't remember any of the nurses or the doctor I saw. I only remember that, at some point, someone told me the on-call psychiatrist had reviewed my case and admitted me for a voluntary forty-eight-hour stay in the psychiatric ward.

Sean reports that the entire visit didn't take too long because the ER wasn't busy that night. Ashley and Sean were quickly separated from me and stayed in a waiting room. They did not say goodbye to me because they thought they would get to see me again, but they did not. A nurse told them that they were going to admit me into the ward. She later came back and said that I was checked in and that they could leave.

Sean felt badly for me and couldn't believe the extreme nature of the situation we were in, but he was also relieved. He had been watching me go downhill, and he knew I wanted help to feel better, so he was glad I was finally getting the help that I desperately needed.

On May 14, Mom journaled: "Ashley H. came to help Jackie. Sean talked to Mike M. Mel H. got Jackie into Sanford. She's so weak and exhausted."

The only way I can really begin to summarize the experience of checking into the psychiatric ward or explain how I felt on May 14 is to play the song "Requiem For a Tower" in the darkness, on repeat. What moves me most about that song is its repetition, but it's also what makes the song horrifying. The way the orchestra plays the same chords over and over, in a dark and dramatic fashion, leaves you feeling like you're trapped inside of something. The chanting in the song is also quite chilling. It's rhythmic, but so soft that it's hard to hear. You can't really make out what the chorus is saying.

Between my shaking, my ears ringing, and my mind starting to fade, I was losing it. And even though I couldn't hear music at that time, it was like that song was repeatedly playing in the background of my life as the soundtrack to my hopeless existence. The situation reminds me of the movie *The Dark Knight Rises*, when Batman tries to escape a prison called The Pit. When Batman looked up above it, he could see light. He believed that he could climb out, even though it looked impossible. And to help him get out, the prisoners rallied around him by chanting. It was hard to get out, if not impossible, for anyone else, but he finally did it.

Prior to leaving work, I could still see some light if I looked up. I felt like with enough hard work I could climb out of my dark place and make it back to the top. Before I checked into the psychiatric ward, I still heard some supportive chanting in my ringing ears, which gave me a glimmer of hope that I would make it out. But as time went on, the light above me grew dim, and the chants became faint. I realized that it was impossible for me to get out of my pit. I was a prisoner in my mind and body. And I had become trapped there in a way that didn't allow me to cry out for help.

CHAPTER 14

My recollection from my voluntary commitment to the psychiatric ward on May 14-16 comes from two places… the memories I have, and the small journal I kept while there.

I knew that my memory alone didn't give a complete picture of my stay, but I lived with it for a year. On the one-year anniversary date of my admission, I read the few pages from my journal. The journal bolstered some of my memories and triggered a few other smaller ones.

I then requested and reviewed the medical records from my stay. Reading the records was very emotional and traumatic for me. It was through them that I learned I was mostly unaware of what was going on around me. My memories were nominal and distorted. I read about myself as a patient being treated for a serious mental breakdown. I saw myself misdiagnosed, in spite of my small pleas for help. I learned about what really went on, and it was heartbreaking. I finally grasped the magnitude of my commitment and how helpless I was while there.

What I did on May 14-16, 2018 was monumental in my life. My situation was grave, and I was in the last place on earth I ever thought I'd end up. The memories should be seared into my mind, but instead there's little there. I'll never know everything that I want to know about my stay.

The memories I have will stay with me forever. Some even haunt me. I was a patient in a psychiatric ward. I wasn't supposed to be there, yet I blamed myself for my commitment. My kids visited me amidst committed patients in matching scrubs in a strange and sterile environment. I'm left to cope with that.

My Memory

I have no memory of being wheeled up to the floor that housed the psychiatric ward. I can only picture a brief moment where I'm sitting in the chair in front of the locked double doors to enter. It was there that someone took my bag and made me take off my running shoes. I was angry that I had to take them off and give them up because I needed those shoes like medicine for my legs. But I acquiesced, knowing it was futile to argue, and my body and mind were already nearly crippled from my exhaustion and undiscovered illness.

I went straight to a room and met with a nurse, Jacob, for intake. Jacob made a lasting effect on me, and I still remember quite a bit of our encounter. He was calm, sociable, and kind. By the time I got to him, I had calmed down a lot. After I was finally admitted, I don't think I cried any more until I went to bed. I think it was because I was so happy to finally be there, to get help, and because I was overwhelmed with fear. The sobering reality that I was a patient in a psychiatric ward immediately set in.

As I sat down in a chair by Jacob, someone brought me some food; a sandwich and something in a container where you peel plastic off the top. It was later in the evening, and I was hungry, so I ate it all. Jacob and I thoroughly discussed my medical history, and I don't believe I struggled to answer his questions. As the experience was unfolding, it felt outlandish. Overall, I had been healthy and successful throughout my thirty-four years of life. Yet, I was suddenly in a small room, in a psychiatric ward, opening up about my rapid onset of severe mental health problems.

I easily denied the many questions about drug and alcohol abuse, yet paused when asked about any suicidal ideations. At any other time in my life, the answer would have been a quick and hard *no*. But I feared I wouldn't receive the help I needed if I wasn't completely open, so I spoke up truthfully. I told Jacob about what I had said to Sean a few days earlier, how a person could desire self-harm after prolonged insomnia. I clearly stated that I didn't believe I would try to hurt myself, nor did I want to hurt myself, but deep down, I assumed that my admission alone would cause concern. I reassured myself it was best to be honest in the environment, and I let it go.

What I remember most about our encounter was what he said to me at the end of the intake: "I know you haven't slept in a while, but this really seems to be medical and not behavioral." It was like he questioned whether I was supposed to be there, and as my time in the ward went on, so did I. In hindsight, the statement was quite astute on his part.

After we finished up, we walked around the ward a little, and then he walked me to my room. The floor was dim and quiet, and I don't remember seeing any other patients. When we arrived at the entrance to my room, he said, "You have a roommate, and her name is 'Jane Doe[6].'" That was it. That was all he said about her.

My mind went wild. I started to panic, and I wanted to bolt. I hadn't considered a roommate during my stay. I already felt on high alert because of the reality of where I was, but then all I could think of was the Law Review article that I authored in law school about civilly committing "the dangerously mentally ill." I questioned this woman's story, but I couldn't even see her. I could only see her back. She was curled up asleep in a bed on the far side of the dark room. I was able to calm myself down by the quick reminder that I had to be there. Roommate or not, I had to suck it up.

Jacob accompanied me into the room to show me a little cubby right off the bathroom that had things for me to use: toiletries, towels, a water bottle, and some comfy, warm socks, since shoes were not allowed. My bag was kept at the nurses station, which was behind glass. The clothes on me, and things provided for me in the room, were all I had. Jacob then left me there, and I was on my own.

Either in the ER, or when I got up to the ward, I was given some medication to sleep. I believe it was Trazadone, at a higher dose than I had been taking before, and Zoloft. I didn't have anything to put away or anything to do, and, without the energy to even brush my teeth, I crawled into my strange bed with my clothes on.

---

6 This is a fictitious name with no relation to an actual person.

The beds in the psychiatric ward aren't luxurious. My recollection is of a flat, narrow twin bed on top of a metal base. The sheets were thin, my pillow was flat, and I had only one light blanket on for a cover. Given how I thrashed at night, I feared I'd fall out.

As I lay alone in the unknown and dark place, I found a little energy to panic and silently cry. I was going to bed for the night in a psychiatric ward, and a stranger was sleeping next to me. And I would wake up the next morning to a "committed" status. Even though I was there voluntarily, the locked doors, the taking away of my shoes, and the overall antiseptic tone made me feel like I had been committed. I thought about how I was a successful trial lawyer who lived in a beautiful home with my family but was now in this most eerie place. A place that didn't even seem to exist in my reality. I had to fight off the despair that plagued me. *How the hell did I end up here?* It couldn't be possible, but it was. Everything around me told me it was real.

I reassured myself that I was in the place that could deliver me help and, hopefully, sleep. I was also very thankful to Ashley, Mike, and Betsy for coming to rescue me and taking care of my kids. I was in awe of what good friends I had. And as awful as it was for me to be where I was, I knew my kids were safe and well taken care of in my absence. But I already missed them and Sean, which only made me cry harder.

* * *

A flashlight woke me up in the morning. I believed I had tossed around a lot and didn't sleep much. I had also felt the flashlight on me throughout the night, which was disruptive. My roommate wasn't in the room, so I got up and decided to face the situation alone. I ventured straight to the main gathering space, where people were congregated for breakfast. I was still wearing my same street clothes from the night before, and everyone around me was wearing red scrubs. Jacob had informed me that I didn't have to wear scrubs because I was a voluntary patient, but I didn't know I'd be the only one. As I entered the open space, I immediately felt the stares and heard some grumblings from others about me not wearing scrubs. I was already different, and it was unnerving, but I let it go.

My breakfast tray was set up with my name on it, so I didn't choose my seat at the table. Whether I sat with anyone, I don't remember. But I think someone told me that the French toast I was eating was the special for the first morning. I vividly recall seeing an elderly man who looked like a typical committed patient in a movie—tired, unshaven, matted hair, pale, and shuffling to walk. I felt empathy for him, but instant fear for me. I began to feel my internal alarms going off—*Oh, my God. I'm in a psych ward!*

My instincts immediately instructed me to keep to myself and not say much to anyone. It was odd because I'm such a social and talkative person by nature, but something told me to just stay quiet and not give out too much information about myself.

Breakfast tasted good, and I ate really well. After breakfast, I walked around a little, but I wondered why no one was doing anything for me. I went to the nurses' window and started crying and asked them to send someone to my room to help me. I went back to my room to cry in my bed. Later, an occupational therapist came in to visit me. I have no recollection of the specifics of our conversation. She sat on my bed with me, and I sobbed. I'm sure I gave her the same litany of no sleep, burnout, and my fault. She comforted me with the assurance that the people there were going to help me. She also had a book in mind that she believed would help, so she went and got it for me. After she gave it to me, she left.

I know I "read" the book on and off in my bed quite a bit for the two days I was there, but I have no idea what it was titled or what it was about. I'm sure I worked hard on it, to try to help myself. But I doubt I was comprehending any of it, and I don't think I got through too much of it.

I think I got a bit more familiar with my roommate on the first day and felt reassured that I wasn't in danger. She wasn't mean, but she wasn't out to make a new friend in me. She was mostly aloof, and I could tell that this stay wasn't her first. She definitely knew her way around and had acquaintances there. If I did ask her something, she was helpful and answered me, but we left it at that. The only real scene I can play back with us together was early on during day one, when she was in the room with me, which was seldom. As I relive it, it's dark and cold in the room, and we're both in a state of tearful despair. I asked her, "Are you a mother?"

All she said was, "Yes."

Then we both cried a little, and that was that.

* * *

At some point, I was invited to my first group therapy session, which was encouraged. I don't know how many sessions I joined over the two days, but I recall two different types. In most sessions, I sat with other patients and staff around a table in a small room where we did verbal or paper exercises. I also participated in creative therapy in what felt and looked like a middle school art room. I mainly crafted by coloring because that was all I could mentally and physically muster. I'm not very crafty on a good day, so asking me to do something creative as a therapeutic measure in the shape I was in just wasn't going to happen, nor help. Attempting to color was difficult because I was so shaky. I could hardly hold a crayon or steady my hand for the gentle back-and-forth strokes.

I also worked on painting two crosses for my kids, but it was strenuous. I recall a pile of blank wooden objects, like you'd buy at the craft store. Whether unconsciously picking the cross in a plea to God, or for ease, I chose crosses. My daughter's is outlined in pink paint, has her initials painted on it, and has a few stones glued to it. I can picture a box of stones and my shaky hands trying to choose and place them on my works. My son's is similar and blue. Both look like they had been crafted by a child. They now sit inside a cupboard in my home office, unsure of their purpose.

In group sessions, people talked about a lot of deep-seated issues and how they knew what they needed to do to stay on track. They all desperately wanted to stay out of the ward. I listened along and felt really badly for them. Even in the dark place I was in, something inside told me that because I was me, and because I had all the tools to be a successful lawyer, I was going to get out of my blackness and never return. It was also during these sessions that I started to seriously question why I was there. I didn't seem to look or act like anyone around me. Everyone was tired, lethargic, quiet, sad, and fairly even keel, in a despondent sort of way. Most people didn't even cry, almost as if they were past that. I bawled all the time, was jittery, and my whole body shook. My feelings, actions, and behavior made me different. And even I could see it.

I tried to stay positive and kind toward others. I hoped that I was going to get better soon and have better days ahead, so I wanted to cheer on others and help boost them too. During one group, a young man was allowed his jeans and white tee because he said he was getting out soon. He talked about past issues with drugs and the law and how he hoped to do better. I spoke directly with him some during that session. And as he left, I gave him a fist bump and told him to take care of himself and stay away from drugs. He seemed genuinely thankful for the encouragement.

Our meals were delivered to the floor via a hospital tray. We were able to order off a paper menu by circling our choices for the day and next morning. I don't remember struggling to choose what I wanted to eat, and I enjoyed the food. I also liked the snack counter that opened in the afternoon. But because I wasn't sleeping, I stayed away from any caffeine. And in an effort to be like Mom, I ordered decaf coffee for all three meals a day. Just like with the necklace I had put together the week before, I was trying to comfort myself with familiarity.

If I wasn't eating, or in a group session, I sat on my bed to try to rest, which never happened. I also read the book the therapist gave me, and I wrote in my little black and white composition notebook, my journal, that was given to me in one of my first sessions. Journaling was encouraged, and I was happy to partake. The only other thing I did was walk the circular perimeter of the floor. I covered the same ground over and over while carrying my water bottle. I was angry that I didn't have my shoes because walking in only my socks hurt my legs, but I needed something to do. There were some newspapers, magazines, television, and movies, but nothing outside of my mundane activities appealed to me. I felt like I lacked desire, not that I understood that I was incapable. Everything took too much energy, so it lacked appeal.

When I left work and began lying on the futon at home and star-ing at the small clock, I realized that I was having some trouble telling time. When I got into the ward, it got worse. As I sat on my bed and looked at the clock on the wall, it jumped around. I also struggled to identify the day and date. That Tuesday morning, the 15th, I sat with my journal and tried desperately to figure out what day it was. I kept trying to write it out and couldn't do it. I told myself that I was supposed to have a trial on Thursday and Friday, May 10-11, and that I was admitted on Monday the 14th. I put all those numbers together under the days of the week and tried to get to the current date, but I couldn't. I wrote T-F-S-S-M; 10-11-12-13-14, but I could not get to Tuesday and to the 15th. I think that raised a red flag in my head, but whether I was able to communicate that or not, I don't remember. In my recollection, if I did tell the providers something, they didn't take it seriously anyway.

There were two phones off of the main gathering area for pa-tients to make local calls. I called Sean quite a bit to say hello and see how the kids were doing. I also called him when I was feeling lone-some and scared, which was a lot. I needed a few things too. I asked him to bring me some more comfortable clothes that I would be al-lowed to wear—ones without strings in them. I remember calling Sean frequently, but I have no recollection of the actual calls. I can picture myself talking to him once while I became agitated at another patient in the ward. I don't remember her until later in my stay. She was a younger gal, with pink dyed hair, who, in my recollection, was always making a scene. She was purposely being obnoxiously loud on the other phone, while staring at me. She was the only patient I strongly disliked. The few times I was near her, but mostly while at the phones, I wanted to punch her. During one of the first calls to Sean, I asked him to use my cell phone to call a friend. I gave him the visitor hours too. I needed a priest.

* * *

In the two days I was in the ward, I actually had four visitors. A priest was my first visitor. He is the Very Reverend Christopher J. Kadrmas, JCL, an old friend.

I really wanted to speak to him in particular. I had known Fr. Chris my whole life. He was also one of the three priests who presided over our wedding. He lived and worked in the Bismarck area, so we were able to catch up now and then, which I always enjoyed. He's kind, tells great stories, and is exceptionally bright. What mostly drove me to ask for his visit was because I knew that he had once taken a break from work while suffering from burnout and depression. We had discussed it upon his return from out-of-state treatment. Because of his personal experience, I believed he could help me. I am also a practicing Catholic, so it felt perfectly comfortable and almost necessary to ask for my priest while there.

Although I adore Fr. Chris, my encounter with him that day elicits very strong and sad memories for me. It was almost like my final day of reckoning. The reality of my presence in the psychiatric ward, because of my own doing, was bursting out of me. It was all my fault that I was sick and committed. I had led myself down this horrible path, and now I had to atone for my sins.

I don't recall who told me I had a visitor. I only remember that I knew he was coming. I believe it was sometime during my first day. I sat and waited for him in a room that felt like a broom closet. It was small and cluttered. When he came in, I gave him a big hug and was happy to see him, but I was crying. I felt like a hot mess and read fear and alarm on his face when he saw me.

While I told him the story leading up to my commitment, I bawled. We then briefly discussed when he was sick. In my memory, he calmly and precisely told me that he had more problems with sleep apnea than he ever did with depression, which made me feel bad about myself. I felt like he didn't want to be associated with me. I was embarrassed and ashamed of where my life had led me.

He asked me if I wanted him to perform two Sacraments of the Church, Confession and Healing of the Sick. I told him, yes, I wanted that very much. What's remarkable about my desire is that even as a practicing Catholic, I hadn't gone to Confession since high school when I was asked to go for Confirmation. I believe that I can clearly communicate my sins to God and feel bad for them on my own. I tried to do that when I often recited a simple Act of Contrition prayer I learned when I was about eight or nine:

> Dear God, I'm sorry for doing wrong. Please for-
> give me all of my sins. I know you love me very
> much. Help me love you in return, and continue
> to care for others as you do. Amen.

But that day, I believed I had to confess my sins to God with a priest. I remember Fr. Chris putting on a purple stole over his black clothing and white collar and then hearing my confession. I cried and was hysterical, similar to how I had acted with Melanie. I told him that everything was my fault. I had turned into a monster, and I had lost all sense of priorities. It was a similar story in that family law had done it to me, but this time I think I added in that I had turned greedy. When we got to the end, Fr. Chris asked me to say my Act of Contrition prayer, and I just shook my head and mumbled, "I can't say it." My mind was blank. I could not recite a simple prayer. He then led me in prayer and performed the Healing of the Sick Sacrament.

I don't remember saying goodbye to him or anything else I told him. The memory of us that I can picture isn't very vivid. I can only see a light overhead, clutter all around, and him sitting in a chair facing me. But I can still feel my strung out and wild emotions. I can feel the pain in my heart, from my blame, and the emotions I believed that I saw on his face.

During my second morning, Sean and the kids visited. I didn't know until long after the fact that Ashley was adamant that Sean not take the kids there to see me and that Mom was hesitant as well. But Sean allowed it because he said it was all I talked about when I called him. He knew I'd be crushed if I didn't get to see them. After I was whisked away Monday night, the kids knew that I was in the hospital because Sean told them that "Mom doesn't feel good." They didn't ask many questions about my stay and were excited when they knew they were going to visit me.

They rode up to my floor in the elevator and had to buzz to be allowed in when they got to the double doors. Then, they waited inside the doors, with a counter surrounded by glass, where Sean signed them in. They were escorted inside by a staffer, through the main gathering area, to a room with a table and chairs and a television and VHS player. They saw other patients in their hospital scrubs on their way in and out.

They waited for me for about ten minutes because Sean believes I was in a session. The kids fiddled with the VHS player, believing it was a DVD player, and began asking questions about the video tapes. They were excited about one of the old Disney movies and asked to watch it. When I came in, I was very happy to see the kids. I frequently hugged them and told them that I missed them. I was able to interact with them and ask them basic questions about their day. Our son showed me the television and told me we could watch a movie together. When my daughter bounced from coloring at the table to sitting by me, I stroked her long, blond hair.

Sean and I mostly interacted by talking about how I felt. I stated that I was doing well, and that because of my stay I was getting better. Sean didn't believe that and wasn't sure that I did either. He saw me trying to convince myself that I was getting better. My physical appearance showed my lack of sleep. I was pale and had dark circles under my eyes. And my behavior was still concerning to him.

Prior to my commitment, I was lethargic. During the visit, he describes me as amped up, like someone had given me a Red Bull, a little out there, and uneasy. I sat nervous and anxious, like something was going to happen to me. It only lasted for about fifteen minutes because I was fidgeting like I needed to go do something to heal myself. Sean felt like they were almost a hindrance to me. Yet when they were leaving, he said I was very sad.

Because the kids were so young, they weren't nervous around me and didn't question the setting or other patients in red pajamas. Our daughter did ask when I was coming home, and Sean could only reply, "When she feels better." After that, she asked if they could go to the park.

I have absolutely no recollection about the visit or when it took place. I merely remember that they were there in that small room. I probably only remember the VHS player because of the kids messing with it. That's really the whole scene in my memory—fluorescent hospital lighting, and an image of the kids crouched down by the television and VCR. I cannot picture Sean. Everything else is a blur, like in a dream, which is really the way I remember much of my time there. Snapshots of time, with light to possibly make out a person, in front of the blur.

* * *

I can't say that I was overly ashamed to be in the ward, but I definitely didn't want anyone to know I was there. I was careful to only say my first name when asked. One time while I was eating, I saw someone in the nurses station behind the glass, and I recognized her as an area social worker whom I had encountered in my work with juvenile cases. What little I knew of her, I didn't like her, because I questioned her professionalism and judgment, and I doubt she cared for me. Thus, I was deathly afraid that she had seen me and she would run to tell people I was in the ward. I hoped that between my hair up and my street clothes, and because I had just turned around briefly, that she didn't see me, and that if she did she didn't recognize me. I walked to the nurses station and asked if a woman named "Janet Doe[7]" was just there. They looked at me puzzled, but said yes, that was her. The fear that she had seen me was real. I became very embarrassed and worried that someday I would be shamed for my commitment. I was able to once again reassure myself that I needed to be there and believed that I would take care of problems in the future, if and when they arose.

I told only one man that I was a lawyer, and his name was "John Doe[8]." I think I first met him at a meal, but I can't remember if he asked me to sit by him or if our trays were placed together. He had a gentle face, he spoke calmly, and I could tell he was very smart. He had long hair and a long beard. He told me that he had once considered law school. I think he could tell that I was scared, so he talked with me quite a bit that day and was very kind. He seemed to be close to my age, or maybe a little older. Given what he was telling me, I understood that

7   This is a fictitious name with no relation to an actual person.
8   This is a fictitious name with no relation to an actual person.

he had been to the ward before. He was the only person, outside of my roommate Jane, whom I remember having a conversation with.

Something that will always stick with me is from one of the group sessions with John Doe. He talked about how his mental illness had negatively impacted his life, and how he knew it would continue on into the future. When I spoke with him and sat by him in the art room, he seemed a little happy, but when he spoke in the session, he was despondent. He said that he knew he'd never get better and that he'd be paranoid and have mental health problems for the rest of his life. It broke my heart, and I remember thinking that it must be awful to feel like that, to believe that you will never get better. The picture of his kind face, our chats, and hearing what he said that day in group is more vivid in my memory, mostly because of how his story made me feel. Even though my life seemed upside down and dark, I still believed that I would get better and work through my issues. I never believed that I had a lifelong debilitating mental illness. I knew something was wrong with me, but I felt very different from what he described. There was still a tiny flicker inside of me that flashed "Jackie M. Stebbins, Stebbins Mulloy Law Firm," while I was losing all control of my voice, brain, and body. Yet my situation was not something I could work through or will away. I was ineffective against what was overtaking me.

I can only now fully grasp my complete loss of agency during my forty-eight-hour stay. It didn't matter that I was a successful and powerful woman outside of those walls. Inside the double doors and behind all the glass, I played by very strict rules in an environment of heavy control and nominal liberty. I had to go to the nurses station to ask for absolutely everything, including my medication. It's my recollection that it was a challenge to receive the one daily prescription I brought with me and anything over-the-counter. I once asked to take three Pepto Bismol tablets, which my GI nurse practitioner recommended for me to take three times a day for my colitis. I feel like it was an ordeal, and they only allowed me two, per a claim that I would otherwise exceed the recommended dosage on the label. It may have registered that I wasn't even allowed to take my diarrhea medication in the way I was accustomed, but I doubt I ever realized that I was powerless.

Yet, I don't believe I made it an issue (although it wouldn't have helped) because my colitis seemed to wane while in the ward. It was as if my brain losing power somehow told my body to not allow itself to lose any energy. I remember using the bathroom in my room, but only because I recall nearly getting caught in the door each time I went in and out. I somehow kept getting jolted by and stuck in the swinging hinges. There was something about that door that kept throwing me, like I was too high on drugs to figure it out.

I had to go to the glass station to ask for clean clothes out of my bag so I could shower and change. I only have a slight image of my shaking through a shower in my bathroom, which was more like a tiny one in a gym, not like the usual hospital bathrooms. Whether I requested my favorite blue mesh shorts, or because that was all that was in my bag, I don't know, but I was told that the strings would have to be cut out before I could wear them. I allowed it because I wanted to wear them. I don't know what I wore with the shorts. And in the two days I was there, I think this was my only shower and change of clothes. I never had pajamas.

I still wear those shorts and always notice that the strings are gone.

* * *

I finally saw the doctor. It felt like it took forever. I didn't remember seeing her until the second day. We met in a little room at a table. It was the usual for me in that I cried and shook while I talked to her. She told me that I was going to be okay. I had just worked so hard I shorted myself out. Her telling me that only reaffirmed my self-blame. She assured me that I was going to get better, but that it would take time. Someone else was with her, but I don't remember her name or title. By the time of my commitment, I really struggled with names.

Through my tears and with my head in my trembling hands, I told her I didn't feel like I belonged there. She responded by saying that it would be different if they had a high functioning and a low functioning unit, instead of just the one unit. I had the wits to articulate that I was out of place, but not enough to recognize that what I was saying and what she was answering were probably two different things.

As I sat through more sessions, and got to the close of day two, I really wanted out. I didn't feel like I was getting the help I envisioned, and I wasn't fitting in. Something kept telling me that I was different and didn't belong there, or that I was there incorrectly. I also didn't believe that the medication and treatment were helping. I had enough and wanted to leave.

I had an enormous appreciation for the pleasant and professional staff and felt like they were very dedicated people. They all exhibited passion and care for the patients. Outside of the obvious of where I was and why I was there, I didn't have any complaints about my stay or how I was treated.

I don't remember Sean and the kids coming to get me, nor do I remember the ride home. I do remember my discharge nurse telling me about my medication, and it confused me. She was a good nurse, but she had a thick eastern-European accent, so it was very hard for me to understand her. When we got home, I panicked and told Sean he had to take me back because I did not think he understood my medication directions and that he had filled my prescriptions incorrectly at the hospital pharmacy. So we drove back to the hospital, called up to the ward, and met with that nurse, who again told us what to do.

In an instant, Sean knew I wasn't any better. The knot in his stomach was still there, and he was afraid to bring me home.

Memories from my Journal

A year later, as I began to read the journal I kept in the ward, I was extremely nervous about what I would find. I expected it to be convoluted and nonsensical, but I was a little surprised. Overall, it was more coherent than I thought.

The first page and a half is from the first day. My penmanship wasn't great, but it's legible. It's done entirely in print form, except for one botched attempt to write "anxiety" in cursive. Normally, my writing is tight and small, and I prefer to use college-rule paper. The work in this wide-ruled notebook is more jagged and sloppy. It's apparent that my hand shook while writing, like a great-grandmother signing her checks.

What's most remarkable about the first page is my obvious struggle with the date. On its top right corner is where I remembered trying to figure out the day and date. I wrote:

T F S S M

10 11 12 13 14

On the top left-hand margin is where I finally arrived at "Day 1/ Tues/May 15." It was a struggle to finally get to May 15, as the 15 is scribbled and written over a number of times. But its placement was normal for me because I routinely wrote the date on the top left margin of any notes I took as a trial lawyer. That was the only date in the journal.

Overall, my stored memories from the first night and morning were pretty accurate. I don't believe that I received this journal until one of my first group sessions, so these thoughts would have been after a session. By the look of it, I wrote all the entries at one time.

> *Admitted last night (Monday* is written directly above this)
>
> By mid afternoon the plan was inpatient—I
>
> had wanted to the week prior but didn't
>
> when Ashley met me in my room I cried really
>
> really hard—cried hard on Mike & Betsy too.
>
> HUG MY BABIES!
>
> Be brave!
>
>
> Woke up to a flashlight and vitals
>
> breakfast was good—the atmosphere is interesting
>
>
> Staff are all so committed
>
> patients keep to themselves but are pleasant

food is good. I liked Jacob my nurse, his
brother went to UND Law. We talked. He was
really surprised at what is going on.

had to go ask Nurse to get someone in my room
this
morning to talk. Jill came the OT & she's nice.

As the afternoon progressed and I got to the second page, my
shaking is worse and the writing is more labored. I think I knew that
my memory was bad, so I was trying to use the journal to store facts
like names and my medication. I'm not sure where I got the times from.

it's like 2:30 pm on Tuesday—I left SM Law Tuesday
at 5pm & completely collapsed from there.
Feels like such an odd set of facts—I SURELY
NEVER UNDERSTOOD!

it's been the perfect middle aged storm—34, 2
kids,
1 hubby, mom and dad, finances, catching up.
Was
I going that strong! BETTER DAYS AHEAD—Good
days

Saw Dr (scribbled out and wrote Carlson? above
it) 3pm Tuesday
nice, smart, beautiful & understood
she literally told me I looked like a ghost

sitting there jumpy.

it is anxiety–(illegible) is a fast pase

Zoloft, melatonin, Benadryl, B_____, D_____

for meds! Will watch for a year–follow up w/
her

After I saw the doctor, I reflected on my level of fault in the situation. I believed that I had so much going on in life that my body and mind just gave out. Once I read the portion about the doctor telling me I looked like a jittery ghost, I remembered it. My shaking was very pronounced. It was part of the reason that I felt like I behaved differently than other patients; that and my incessant crying.

I couldn't remember the doctor's name. At some point, I figured out her name and clearly wrote *Ashley Crawford* in the left margin, next to where I had incorrectly called her *Carlson?*. I struggled to remember the names of the other providers there too. To the right of my entry about the doctor, I wrote the names and titles of the people I was seeing.

(met w/ Jill OT, Brenna M.D.

Scott, OT Jacob, RN [9]

Day two begins at the bottom of the second page and goes on for six more full pages. The writing during the second day matches the mania that Sean saw in me. It's shakier, forced, and sometimes illegible. It's also not as logical to follow as I go back and forth in the time of day. I would equivocate it to when you're dreaming and you believe that you're doing something routine that makes sense to you in that dream, but not when you awaken. Or if you would leave yourself a late-night note, while intoxicated. It makes perfect sense at the time, but little sense when you attempt to read it the next day. It's obvious that I couldn't do what I wanted so badly to be able to do, which was express myself through writing. I wanted to heal myself. I was also trying to pass the time.

---

9 I learned years later that my nurse's name was actually Jason.

I attempted to write two sentences in cursive, but it's barely legible. I wrote with a sense of purpose, like it was work to put out each letter and place words together. I made a few direct references to the time, but the rest of the time is made more vague by my use of morning or afternoon.

My review of the entries from the second day didn't give me much independent recollection of my stay, just powerful feelings of my decline. I believe I began writing after I ate breakfast.

Wednesday May 16 Day 2–feels tough–so shakey–waking

up confused–went to bed after dinner & shower last night after

slept more I think–which is good.

What is the problem, what is my diagnosis?

Why do I feel like this–ugh–its scary!!!

Miss my mom, miss my kids so bad, tough here

but I may have to make it bust out after.

-yesterday mouth sore, jaws sore, shakey, fatigue

-tired & restless–just want to turn a corner.

Dear god thank you for my blessings!

Please guide me through this.

Talked to Ashley this am at like 10am, her

and my M.D. student

it came on–so much work & so much stress

After talking to the doctor
I feel so much better! Better Days Ahead!

Leaving on a jet plane!
seeya after this summer!

I struggled to conclude the entry. I think I was trying to verify my memory by reciting what I ate for breakfast and had for snacks.

Foo D Here

Food

breakfast was so good, french tst, 1st am & bacon
Pancakes, sausage 2nd am

-Sckacks
-sandwiches, fruit, decaf coffee
-drinks, sherbet, Powerade
be so hungry & do virtually nothing–feels
like an empty stomach all day so eat!

The next entry was probably written after I finished my art, and it stands alone.

Morning #2: 11am
OT group I painted

The next entries begin at the top of a page and are from a group session or maybe multiple sessions. I think I was writing what others were sharing because the thoughts don't sound like mine. It would be my nature to try to take copious notes, as I'm an active learner. That would have been in my head, along with the faint knowledge that I was struggling to follow along and remember. Every few words, my writing goes from sloppy to legible for the duration of the page.

Day 2: early afternoon

-group

-parallel – group conscious–busy happy hands
goal, self, mindful

dial back a (scribble) bit-& catch it!

I've been bottling up (scribbled hard over just keeping)
withdrawing
when you cope well you make adjustmet

faith helps! Keep the faith

stuck–drug-out–not going anywhere
make your changes, once you think it through & make your
chances–keep your meds–keeps stability

existing in life–that's all–barely–get the
bad thoughts out of your mind
he's different–he knows it
I catch give away my strength until nothing left for me!

Next to these entries, I jotted down in the left margin "stop & close your eyes for 60 secs." In one of the sessions while we were working on an exercise, I recall becoming emotional and upset, so one of the staff asked me to just stop and close my eyes. I was crying really hard, and I remember thinking *what the hell is this going to do for me?* But I did it.

What's noticeably absent in these pages, is anything about my family and Fr. Chris visiting me. The only real reference to my children is in my early morning entry. I wrote my daughter's name with a heart and my son's name with a word that looks like "lard," but I assume it meant "love."

The next page begins my final afternoon. My writing is mostly legible. The top left margin begins the entry with "Wed afternoon."

chest sore, fatique, shakey, tremor

light, floating–it is all so much!

parrellell pm–colored a few pics

-got some meds @ (crossed out and over 2 and 3) pm

read the newspaper–laughed at DT (Donald Trump)!

I hate DT!

Pray for forgiveness (but it's all scribbled out)

ALWAYS LOVE

All U Need is loved

Let it be!

7 Pillars of Wellness at UND–that's your well-ness

you have to be so well rounded out in

each (looks like patrg.)

spirit, mind, sight, sound, touch, listen

thought,

Whether it was the medication, or the later time in the afternoon, the writing on my final page is about the worst of my penmanship. It's hard to make out; 3pm is written on the top left-hand margin.

just about snack, I read, did a group & rested

a little shaoky today so at about 2pm some

benadryl to (illegible)

been a challenge on Earth

it's obvious that I got this—but I was

not listening &

I was

lying to myself

I think I just hate for family Law is so damn

emotional, ragged & angry! I didn't (illegible) it (illegible)

I do want out! That's my (illegible) for life. I want (illegible but I think I'm trying to write balance).

48 hours/ Rescue 9-11/ 60 Mins/ Mash

gave me the sleeping willies I need to stay

very positive—I don't want to be afraid

to sleep! That was the (illegible but I think it says worst).

Everyone is more scattered today

Trainstran smoothly today

Behind, late, missed some of the 7 (illegible Pillars)

4. Could someone feed me, take me home &

get me well. Could I be healed like magic!

That's the last of the journal entries from the ward. I did want to be healed like magic, and I wish it would have worked that way.

The Medical Records

After I reviewed my medical records, I didn't feel any better about my rare illness. The presentation of the symptoms during my onset really was confusing. I articulated a few thoughts about my bizarre state to the staff, but it wasn't enough. I wish my behavior and those few thoughts could have translated into more providers questioning whether my problems were medical. I don't fault anyone because the disease is sneaky. And overall, I'm sure much of what I was saying and doing did look like mental health issues—because I walked and talked like someone who had shorted out from anxiety.

In the ER, I was first examined for drugs and alcohol. They performed a routine screen for barbiturates, benzodiazepines, amphetamines, THC, cocaine, and opiates, when I've never done a drug in my life, including smoking or eating pot.

Based upon my physical exam, the ER physician noted I was oriented to person, place, and time. My neurological exam showed me alert and oriented to person, place, and time, with normal reflexes.

My chief complaint for my admission was insomnia. I reported that my lack of sleep began in November and worsened through the following six months. I reported that I hadn't slept in the last three days. I felt "unsafe" at home and was concerned about my ability to care for my children. I repeatedly stated that my symptoms had gotten to the point of becoming quite dysfunctional. I met the criteria for psychiatric admission based upon my inability to function on a daily level, my insomnia, and my concerns for safety.

Hospital records indicate: "Patient was admitted to the psychiatric unit and placed on fifteen-minute checks for suicide precautions and safety." People were waking me up with flashlights that first night. I was on suicide watch. The records show me consistently denying suicidal ideations in the past or present, but I'm sure my admission of what I previously said to Sean placed me on the watch.

The first medical provider I saw during my stay was a physician's assistant. I stated to her probably the most profound and powerful few words of my commitment—"I feel like I'm going crazy." I did feel like I was "going crazy," and I was desperate for help. But I was in a unit that couldn't help me.

I reported that I was struggling to shut my mind off before bed and that I had racing thoughts. I felt like I was thinking about nothing, yet about everything, all at the same time. It probably sounds nonsensical, but it makes sense to me because I can somewhat recall the dark contrasting feeling. There was absolutely nothing of substance in my mind. But the fear of what was taking over my being remained, and it pulsated through me.

I told her I felt like I was going to have a panic attack. I woke up from sleep with shortness of breath and sweats. I had crying spells and thoughts of hopelessness and guilt. I also had increased fatigue and difficulty concentrating. Thus they believed I had a panic disorder.

I was very open about all the stressors I felt in my life and how I believed they had negatively impacted me and left me in the state I was in. I reported that I had increased work stress for the past three years since starting my own law firm and that I was having difficulty turning off extra responsibilities and projects. I was worried about Dad's health and my parents' future. I told her that I had worked out the prior week until the symptoms increased to the point where I could no longer exercise, nor could I even complete daily functions.

I was noted to be well-groomed and appropriate in my clothing and hair style. I was polite and cooperative, but tearful during the interview when I spoke of how dysfunctional my symptoms had become and about my ongoing struggle for months. The provider felt my thoughts were appropriate to my mood but noted that I had to concentrate to recall certain events. She described my mood and affect as tearful and anxious. I was diagnosed with generalized anxiety disorder, panic disorder, and adjustment disorder with depressed mood.

I don't think I ever had a hold on what medication they prescribed for me, but it wasn't very complicated. I continued on Zoloft for depression, and she also started me on BuSpar, an anti-anxiety medication. I was also given Trazadone to sleep. Something I only vaguely remember being prescribed was Propanolol, to help me stop shaking. I had to go to the nurses station to ask for it when I felt like I needed it. I believe that's what I referenced in my journal as Benadryl.

I remained willing to stay in the hospital voluntarily to be monitored for sleep and any medication adjustments. I continued to deny suicidal ideations and agreed I wasn't a harm to myself or others, thus the fifteen-minute checks were discontinued on me after the first night.

* * *

A long time after the fact, Fr. Chris and I discussed his visit with me at the ward. It was a conversation that I was hesitant to have, for fear of what he would tell me. I was nervous and a little embarrassed for him to recount to me what he had witnessed that day.

Fr. Chris reported that we were in a patient room that was being used for storage. It was hard for the staff to find us a place to meet because I was very adamant that I wanted privacy for his visit, but the staff had to be able to supervise. This room was apparently the compromise. He recounts that the place was uncomfortable for both of us.

What was most remarkable to him that day was the deep-seated exhaustion that he could see in me. He didn't believe that I was having a complete psychiatric breakdown because he didn't think that my age and situation fit such a diagnosis. He also saw periods of lucidity that didn't fit with where I had landed. He describes me as jittery and hyperactive, and also tearful.

He discussed with me the nature of being in a psychiatric ward and that he understood how I felt because he could see that I was scared to be there. He has a vast academic background, including occupational therapy, and is very intelligent. While he was an occupational therapist resident, before he was ordained as a priest, he worked in an inpatient psychiatric ward. Ten years after he became a priest, he endured his own struggles with sleep and depression and had voluntarily hospitalized himself in a psychiatric unit. He had personally witnessed both sides of the coin and tried to convey that to me. He told me to listen to my doctors and that they would help me find a path back to better health. He tried to convey to me that my exhaustion and other problems might be medical in nature and that mental health was possibly not the reason I didn't feel well. He wasn't seeing the mental health issues I believed I had and questioned whether I had a medical diagnosis.

It now makes sense to me that, in my state at the time, I believed he was only talking about sleep apnea and "hiding" from depression. I always assumed that my recollection of our conversation that day was skewed. It was.

A month after his visit with me in the ward, he found out that I had been diagnosed with autoimmune encephalitis. He immediately referenced a book he had previously read, *Brain on Fire*, and believed it all made perfect sense.

* * *

Sometime in the evening of the second day, I met with my physician's assistant to be discharged. I have no memory of meeting with her, discussing the discharge, or doing any type of discharge examination. I again told her that my symptoms were so dysfunctional that I felt like I couldn't do daily life. The provider agreed and said it was "noticeable" to her.

I was noted to be tremulous throughout my hospitalization. I had a fast rate of speech, and my anxiety was palpable by the medical staff.

I would often go on tangents. I could answer questions linearly, but the staff felt that I became tangential because my anxiety was so high. I became tearful when discussing how dysfunctional my symptoms were and how badly I felt.

I participated in the occupational groups but was notably anxious and had a fast rate of speech during discussions. The providers believed that was due to my anxiety and racing thoughts. My speech was fast but wasn't pressured and was easily interrupted. I was unable to close my eyes briefly or for a full minute when asked to. This is different from what I remembered about being asked to close my eyes and breathe for a short amount of time. I thought I could do it when I was asked to.

I debated all day during the second day whether I should stay or go. That contradicts what I had in my journal, that I was ready to "bust out." I was given the option to remain in the hospital or be discharged, and I "spent the majority of the day pondering as [I] struggled to make decisions." The provider believed my problem with making decisions was a clear sign of my anxiety and depression. She felt my depression revolved around my anxiety. The more dysfunctional I became, the more anxious I became, which in turn made me depressed.

I elected to be discharged from the hospital and told the provider that I would be able to use the skills I had learned there to help cope with my anxiety at home. My discharge diagnosis remained the same as my admission diagnosis.

I was willing to take time off of work and planned to have Mom help us with our kids. During those two days, I don't remember ever having any thoughts about work, the law firm, going back to work, or not having any income. From a few notes in my journal, I must have discussed my absence from work and mentioned that I had disability insurance, but I don't remember any of the conversations. I don't know if the reality of our monthly bills that I had always taken care of ever registered with me. Had I even tried to open my laptop or use the internet to pay a bill, I would have failed.

I reported that Mom, Sean, and Lacie were all supportive of me, and I agreed to do a follow-up with outpatient care. Thankfully I agreed to do so because that was the appointment set with Nurse Practitioner

Stephanie Macdonald almost a week later, and without Stephanie, I believe I would have been sent back to the psychiatric ward, and I would have either suffered permanent brain damage or I would have died. I was rapidly deteriorating.

In "Requiem for a Tower," most of the four-minute song is a repeating overture of wailing violins, clashing cymbals, and dark, rhythmic chanting. But at minute 1:40 it slows down, as if it will stop. For about ten seconds, the song is pure devastation and despair. It's as if the song is just going to quietly give up on itself.

In the soundtrack of my existence, when I crawl into bed at the ward that first night, I'm at minute 1:40 in the song. I believed that was the darkest point of my life. My mind was nothing more than devastation and hopeless despair, and my mind and body were both giving up on me because they could not go on. I doubt I believed it could get worse, but it did. I just didn't know it because I went further into my dark and lonely place of sickness and despair. The last few futile attempts I made to recognize my life and be a part of it vanished when I left the ward.

My memory goes mostly blank from the night of my release from the ward until I have a few small memories on May 22, when I met Stephanie.

Me on our farm near Bowman in about 1987.

Stebbins and Mulloy in August 2017 © Jackie M. Stebbins
and Micheal A. Mulloy

Me with our daughter on May 7, 2018, at her kindergarten
open house.

Me with our son on May 8, 2018, just after I left work.

Me and Mom on Mother's Day in Bowman, May 13, 2018.

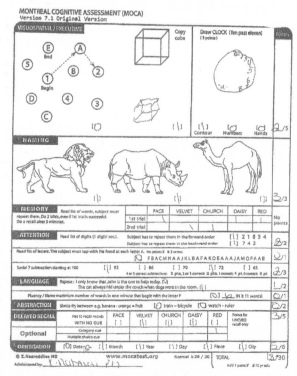

The clock I attempted to draw for a neurological examination on May 23, 2018.

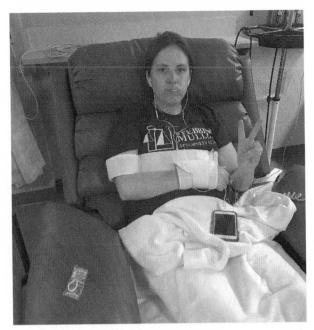

Me receiving my second dose of intravenous steroids at
Mid Dakota Clinic in Bismarck, on June 6, 2018.

Me with Sen. Heidi Heitkamp on October 31, 2018, in Bismarck.

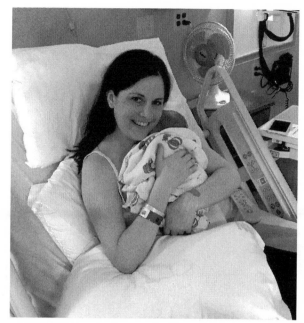

Me with my miracle post-AE baby, on April 3, 2020, at
CHI/St. Alexius Hospital, in Bismarck.

Sean and I still dancing in June 2021. Photo credit: Hannah Photography
© Jackie M. Stebbins

CHAPTER 15

While I was in the psychiatric ward, I missed my family, and I figured they missed me. I had no idea they were all a little relieved that I was in there. Sean's night stress was alleviated because he could finally sleep without my thrashing around in bed, waking up, wandering, and hallucinating. Yet his relief made him feel guilty. He also felt badly that he somehow missed something leading up to my becoming so sick. He desperately hoped that I would get the help I needed at the ward and that life would get better.

Mom was somewhat comforted, too, because she knew that I was fraught with my lack of sleep and that I required assistance to get back on the right path. She journaled on May 15: "Jackie is at the Sanford Psych ward. Sean is relieved she's there, me too. So worried about her."

But Sean felt no reprieve when he picked me up on the evening of the 16th, when he immediately realized that I wasn't any better. He immediately felt the existing knot in his stomach wrenching again. I was not even the same person he had dropped off. I was worse. He quickly reported back to Mom. She wrote: "Jackie's home, Sean needs some help."

* * *

Mom and Dad came to stay with us from May 17-19. On May 17, Mom journaled: "Jack & I went to Bis at 8am to help Sean & be with Jackie. She looks good but she feels like a shell–so hard to see her so sick. She's on 5 meds." On May 18, she wrote: "So glad we're with Jackie & Sean. It

141

means a lot to them. Even tho we can't do anything but listen & encourage her. She's shaky and short-term memory bad. Her appetite is good."

I have some writing in my psychiatric ward journal from those two days. I think I went back to the advice of my counselor friend, and I knew the importance placed upon journaling in the psychiatric ward, so I wanted to keep it up. It was hard for Sean and Mom to watch me try, because it was apparent that I couldn't write anymore and that it was only frustrating me, but I kept trying. I was obsessed with writing or doing some type of self-help work, like I had done in the ward. I even asked Sean to call the ward to see if they could provide him with some exercises for me to do at home. Neither Sean nor Mom believed me to be capable of the exercises that I talked about doing. They could only watch me struggle with what I thought I needed to do and try to redirect me.

On May 17, probably in the morning, my black ink went to blue, and I continued on from where I left off in my ward journal. The style and struggle of my writing is fairly consistent with the entries during my hospitalization.

> Wed. evening release about 5pm
>
> had a good dinner & felt good about going home.
>
> 48-hours is kind of a JMS (scribble) timeframe
>
> talked to Jane Doe quite a bit before I left.
> hopepfully she does well & gas-happy
>
> After 48-Hours
> -I understand that something happened to me & I
> couldn't help it
> -Your mind starts shorting out after some much stress,

product, physical product

TODAY I FEEL LIKE AN ODDER human Better
days ahead

In the same ink, I began on the next page:

Resting at home:

Sleeping on the couch (I had quit that in Jan.
2018 couldn't slep

actually falling asleep!

calm & reasonable breathing

cool, rain, dreary, magic too, smells nice!

In a change back to black ink, and probably in the afternoon as I worsened, I concluded:

NaTURE (scribbl)

cool, damp, rain, smells nice, beautiful sight,
NO, sun

WIND – some what have

outside shoes & my luck

Random "K" letters begin to pop up on these pages, probably for my children's first names.

I also started writing again in the journal that I had started at home, prior to the ward, and I wrote a few things on the 17th and after.

May 17, 2018

home from 48 hours–a JMS plan–go hard

at 48-hrs–then go home & know you can

cope & do well

I want solid progress each day for 14 days!

6:30–May 17th

my lip & mouth feel; like they have been
tingling

-ate well today–thank God for dad and mom!
orange sherbet
pecan delight (drew a heart) too

On the 18th, I ironically asked Mom to write for me in my psychiatric ward journal. "I am writing for Jackie, as she has the shakes today. We did go to Barnes and Noble to look at self-help books, activity books, etc. Jackie got 'Success Affirmations,' by Jack Canfield."

I don't remember much about being at Barnes and Noble. I wore a sack pack on my back as my purse. I vaguely remember walking a few aisles in search of books, but I felt awful the whole time. I could barely stand in the store because I was so weak. And I couldn't tolerate being out in public.

Per Sean and Mom, I was determined to find self-help books and some type of activity books I could work on to better myself. I was upset when we couldn't find much. The book I purchased that day has sat in my bookcase untouched ever since.

I couldn't write in my journal, but asked Mom to do it for me, as if it would somehow help me. And I doubt I could read or comprehend much, but I wanted to buy a self-help book. Life was cruel. And ironic.

I attempted some writing later that day in my psychiatric ward journal. I began in blue ink just under Mom's entry.

Be positive

Went outside

rain

walk

hna

The next page is still in blue ink and is dated May 18. The entry is challenging to read and decipher, and some of it is just gibberish.

> Friday morning Stebbins family here! (drew a heart)
>
> ROYALE Wedding. Harry & Megan
>
> -mom is (illegible) it & (illegible)
>
> hats, the scarves, everybody does (illegible) ver nice.
>
> had chocolatete ice cream
>
> Read u nice note—Betsy journal
>
>
> (scribbles) Ate lunch, sownawndwich
>
> great family! We are (illegible)
>
>
> MOVE + down HOT MIKE

May 18 was a Friday, but the Royal wedding was on the 19th, so I was either writing about the hype on television or my entry date was incorrect. The reference to Betsy's journal comes from a card and gift she left me the night I was checked into the ward. When I got home, a gift bag and card were sitting on my desk. I opened the card and tried hard to read it, but couldn't because it was written in cursive. I had to have Mom read it to me. I knew the journal she gave me was a gift, but it was almost like I couldn't fathom doing anything with it. It was new and unknown to me, so I think I just put it in my bookcase.

Apparently, I drove Mom to run an errand that day. I told Mom and Sean that I was fine to drive, and I did it. We were only at the store for a few minutes so Mom could return something there. I remember being very fatigued. I don't remember anything from the drive except making one right turn onto a busy street.

I was incredulous when they told me I drove after being hospitalized. I thought it happened right after I left work, the week prior. I couldn't believe they let me drive. Sean reported that I wasn't belligerent about it, but I was close, and that I also wasn't yet at the lowest point he had seen me, so he allowed it. Mom just kind of went with it too. This is probably the only time during my onset that I was allowed to do something so dangerous and where I had no concept of my boundaries. Thankfully, I wasn't allowed to take any risks after that. May 18, 2018 was the last time I drove until January 2019.

Mom and Dad went home in the afternoon on the 19th. That evening, Mom journaled: "Watched the Royal wedding. Jackie watched on and off. She wants to feel better so bad!"

On May 19, I wrote in black ink:

> Let's have a good & big day!
>
> I will have energy soon! Swim & bike
>
> bike around the block
>
> do the grapevine
>
> down to the
>
> PERFECT DaY:
>
> -just be alive
>
> All is that I love

I then skipped over a few pages and started writing again in black.

> May 2018, spring, cold windy, we are all
> at home
>
> seems like summer
> lake weather
> sledding hills in the (illegible)

What am I doing, (illegible) it is some of those
& (illegible)

lathat's at a (illegible)

The next page contains some writing and pictures, all in black ink, and is hard to follow.

Get GeRB GRIC-D

RoyG-BivP

depression is deeb

oranges apples & (illegible)

I miss

There are some small doodles in the middle of the page. I drew boxes, lines with circles, and I scribbled. I'm not an artist, and I'm not one to draw, so I'm not really sure why I attempted to doodle. I think I was trying to have busy, happy hands like they taught us in the ward. I think I was also trying desperately to put anything I could on paper, since writing was getting harder for me. I was trying to convince myself that I could still do it. I would journal to get better, no matter what it took.

At the bottom, I wrote the date of May 19, 2018, my age, height, and my initials. I also tried to write my name in cursive, and it looks nothing like my signature. I knew I couldn't write in cursive, but I kept trying.

On the back of that page, but in blue ink, are only two words, and more drawing. I tried to play Tic Tac Toe with myself, marking all the boxes with all Os and one also with an X. I drew a football, a basketball, and what I believe is a volleyball. I scribbled and crossed things out. I wrote the word "doodle" next to a shaky looking cube. On the bottom right, I drew and scribbled, and right next to it I wrote "FUCK."

The last page is in blue ink. The entry ends my psychiatric ward journal.

MOODS

grey–ulgly–(scribble)

icky–*how* (illegible) wish it (illegible) leave!

My first journal contains one last page from this time, and I believe it was written on May 19. It's written in black and blue ink. In the top left-hand corner, I played a game of Tic Tac Toe with myself, wherein I made some extra marks in the squares. On the right side, I wrote:

Friday

rainy

cool

jaws hurt, I'm,

tired. I'm (scribble)

(scribble)

ears ding

head empty

legs are tired–

arms tired

The last section, before I skip two pages and conclude, is in blue ink.

lot of talking to myself in my sleep today

strong shakey feeling today

The conclusion is dated Sunday, May 20:

sleep at night is odd. I believe come & go

a lot.

my king bed will be the death of me

covers, ratty, thrashing, shakey, tight chest

I think I do sleep though

Right near the end, I concluded a page with a thought:

I don't have a lot going for me if I (illegible) away.

CHAPTER 16

Sean describes the six days between my getting out of the psychiatric ward through the date of seeing Stephanie for the behavioral follow-up appointment as the longest and worst year of his life.

His days with me felt endless. In his opinion, everything around me bothered me, confused me, or scared me. He began to worry that I had dementia or that I was going crazy. He felt guilty, but he wanted to just grab me, shake me, and say: *Come on, Jackie, you are an intelligent woman!* He desperately wanted me to snap out of it.

He couldn't leave me by myself. If he left the house, Lacie had to come and watch me. He also didn't ever leave the kids alone with me. I could not walk by myself or stand by myself. I had to hold his arm to walk, and he had to tie my shoes. I could only sit in the bathtub to try to take a quick bath, as I was too weak and shaky to shower. I would mostly just rinse off. I didn't use much shampoo or soap because I was unable. My entire body shook.

If he did take me anywhere, he asked me to stay in the car, and I complied. When we got in the car to take my daughter to school, I asked him, "Where are we going?"

When the kids would say, "Watch me," I just stared and didn't respond to them. It was very hard for me to be around the kids because they nearly tripped me if they got too close. If I was out for a walk, the kids bothered me, and so did any other people or neighborhood dogs.

Sean believes that, to some degree, I knew I was a mess because I was adamant that I didn't want anyone to come to the house, and I specifically did not want anyone to see me.

I was easily confused, and I did abnormal things. I said, "This looks weird," or "Why can't I do this?" about routine objects and tasks. Right after I got out of the ward, Sean asked me what I was doing, and I told him I was doing my laundry. When he went upstairs to check on me, I had put my clean underwear on the floor beneath my dresser and was putting my sweats and shorts in and around the sink in our bathroom.

Once, as I sat in my recliner and my legs were shaking badly, I told him I couldn't feel them.

I thought my phone looked "weird," and I kept commenting to him that something was wrong with it, because the screen was green. When he looked at it, everything was fine. I also texted Lacie and Betsy some odd things about seeing them when I hadn't. Sean finally took my phone away from me. When I no longer had my cell phone, I picked up our landline phone, believing it was my cell phone. I tried to text from it, but could not do so, so I asked Sean to help me. He remembers almost losing it with me at that moment.

I quit using Ambien when I went into the ward, but the nights continued to bring out my worst demons. According to Mom and Sean, my sleeping was like something out of a horror movie. Prior to getting sick, I always went to sleep on my side and hardly moved at all through the night. During this time, my sleeping behavior was re-markable. If I allowed Sean to put any covers on the bed, they ended up mangled all over the bed or on the floor. A few nights, I didn't want any bedding, because I told him that the sheets were burning me. He had to completely strip the bed and try to find blankets I would agree to use. I mostly just wanted my afghan.

Sean witnessed me sleeping upside down, horizontally, and every which way in between. While I thrashed around, I yelled or talked very loudly in gibberish. When he was in the living room on the main floor, he could easily hear me talking in my sleep while I was in my bed upstairs.

Sean took only one short video of me during this time, and it was on May 21. I was speaking so loudly in bed that it was unnerving to him. He went upstairs to film me, but as he got to the bedroom, I quit.

The alarm clock next to me shows that it's 8:17 p.m., and I'm asleep on my back. There are no sheets on the bed, just a blanket wound up beneath me on the mattress pad, and I'm under my afghan. My right hand is up by my head, and after I move it a few times I place it on my pillow. But during the course of the twenty-six second video, I repeatedly clench my left hand to grab at my coarse afghan. He said it was common for me to grab and stroke my afghan at night.

He recalls being disturbed as he tried to sleep in the next bedroom with the kids. In his words, he hardly slept, and if he did, he slept with one eye open. He mostly lay there looking at our beautiful children and wondered what he was going to do in life when I was gone. At first, he was frustrated with my behavior, but then he began to worry that I was going to completely lose my mind or die, and he was terrified of both.

He remained thankful for our home security system and repeatedly tried to reassure himself that he would hear me if I attempted to leave at night. He knew I would set off the alarm because there was no way I could disarm it in my state. He firmly believed that if I got out of the house, I would die. I shiver to think of what could have happened.

I have no recollection of anything, except a little from when I thought my phone was shorting out and distorted. It did look green to me. I don't remember him taking it away from me or how I reacted. He claims I didn't put up much of a fight to stop him, but a few times I acted angry about it and told him, "I'm not stupid."

He could only reply, "I know that, Jackie, but you're not in a good place right now."

I don't remember thrashing around or talking in bed, but I remember feeling confined and paralyzed. Because I was so weak, I felt like anything on the bed, especially covers, trapped me. I felt like I couldn't move or adjust my pillow. At some point, my sister-in-law, Kelly, sent me a weighted blanket, which is a heavy blanket that's supposed to help alleviate anxiety. I was too weak for the actual weighted part but liked the soft outer shell. I'm not sure if it was that blanket or another one on my bed, but I remember feeling like I was bound, and I could not move my covers away from me.

I wish I had a journal, or a video, or a truly accurate depiction of my two recurring dreams during these six days. Never before in my life have I had recurring nightmares or even recurring dreams, but I had two regularly recurring dreams somewhere in those six days, and they terrified me. They weren't scary, per se. No one was chasing me or killing me. I didn't die, and there weren't any similarities from my hallucinations. They just kept happening exactly the same, and they kept frightening me. I don't have any recollection of telling Mom or Sean about them while they were happening, and Mom and Sean don't have any recollection either from that time. The first they remember hearing about the dreams was when I talked about them after I started to get my wits back.

The dreams felt endless, just like the feelings of being paralyzed and trapped in my bed. It was like everything played on repeat, night after night, for what felt like an eternity. I would wake up terrified and try to move, but I couldn't. I was trying to physically get away and stop the dreams, but I couldn't do either. I'm not sure which dream came on first, but they both seemed to play in my mind with similar frequency.

The first dream is my going to a house in South Dakota. It's dark outside and nighttime, but I can see the house. It's a nice home on the outskirts of town. Then suddenly, I'm in the basement, and it's dimly lit. The lights on the walls and in the hallways are like old lights hanging in an ancient castle. I'm alone there. The basement is like a Scheels store. There are relic, steel knight statues posed all around, and there are stand-up punching bags, with sports memorabilia on them. The knights are like the ones I envision in the castles in the Harry Potter books, and the punching bags have NBA jerseys on them. There are also some deer mounts on the walls. While I'm downstairs, I'm waiting for a group of middle-aged couples to come back. I don't know any of them, but they're bringing me something. They're coming in from town, and I think the town is Rapid City. The waiting is really hard for me, and it makes me anxious. At some point, I can hear people in the house. When they start coming down the stairs, it scares me.

I have much less of a memory of my second dream, but I think it scared me even more than the first one. I'm in Bowman, and I'm looking in the trunk of a guy's car. His name is Mike. There's a girl there, too, and her brother. I know of these people because they once lived in Bowman. Three big trash bags are in the trunk. I believe they contain infinity, yet it's all junk, like the stuff you buy in bulk from Oriental Trading. There are tons of paper shreds and mice poop in there.

That dream just kept coming, and I tried to get away from it, because something about the infinity scared me badly. But because I was so paralyzed in my bed, it was like I couldn't wake up enough to move, to get away from it, so I just kept going back to that trunk.

I never had the dreams before, and thankfully, I've never had them again while sleeping. I know I'm not really describing them in much detail, but it's all I can remember. I cannot explain these dreams, *but I can feel them*. If there is one thing in particular that can take me back to the mood of this most awful time in my life, it would be these recurring dreams. I still have daily glimpses of them. It's mostly when it's dark outside or I'm in an area with dim lighting, but they can come over me during the daytime in sunlight. The dreams elicit such strong feelings for me, almost as if they're memories of something that happened.

I often scared Sean at night by coming out of nowhere. When he would walk up our staircase, he would find me standing at the top of the staircase in the darkness, waiting for him. Sometimes I would just appear in the living room while he was watching television late at night before going to bed. By this time, I was as pale as a ghost and had lost weight. I also didn't speak much. He would look up, and I was just there. I imagine myself looking like the pallid-faced doll whose head spins around in a horror movie.

One of the worst memories Sean has starts with me waiting for him in the dark, at the top of the stairs. I was extremely worried, scared, and anxious, and I was telling him that "he" is in here, "he's in the house."

Sean had to repeatedly ask me, "Who?" And then I said his name, "Jim Doe[10]."

Sean remembered his name, because he was once opposite me in a case, and I warned Sean about him because I believed him to be

---

10 This is a fictitious name with no relation to an actual person.

155

dangerous. I had the trial just before I started to get sick, and he raised the hair on my neck.

In our room, I pointed to the corner where our garment steamer sits and told Sean, "He was just standing there, with a gun, and was trying to kill me."

I was convinced that Jim Doe was in the house and that he was going to hurt us. Sean tried to reassure me that no one was in the house and, if so, he would have set off the security system, but I would not hear of it. I made him walk around to every corner of our two-story home, and I creepily followed him. He even had to open every door in the basement and turn on every light so I could verify that "he" was not in the house.

I only vaguely remember thinking that he was in our house, and I remember standing behind Sean looking in the furnace room, but that's about it. I know I was very scared and genuinely believed he was in our home to hurt us.

I think I was convinced of his presence because at some point during that time I had also hallucinated about him. The memory is short and poignant. He was standing behind our twin oak bedroom doors, and when he opened them I sat up in bed, and he shot me at point blank range. He was wearing a white suit like they wore in Miami Vice. The blast of fiery orange and red and powder exploded in my face. When I dreamed it, I don't know whether I really woke up or sat up, but I know it jolted me from my sleep and terrified me. Believing that he was in my house to harm me and my family was much worse.

* * *

Sean didn't talk to Mom much about my behavior after she visited when I got out of the ward. He internalized his emotions and fears, probably in a state of denial. He was also worried that he was possibly wrong about my behavior and that if he told others they'd think he was missing something or that he was just being dramatic. He felt like the few times he did mention to Mom that something was really wrong with me, she didn't seem too shook up.

Mom's recollection is that for the longest time, she clung to the notion that it would take time for my medicine to work. Sean tried hard to believe that as well. But as I got worse, he let go of that notion and believed something else was seriously wrong with me. Mom then also changed her position and believed that I was probably overmedicated, and that was causing my issues.

What was so odd and frustrating to both Mom and Sean during this time was that I had fleeting moments of normalcy, and from time to time I acted fine. It was almost hard for them to get a continuous reading on me because I was so in and out of it. I would act odd and have strange problems, but in the next moment I would come back and act normal.

I was very compliant and didn't get angry with them when I didn't understand or when they treated me like a child. I didn't argue much with them either, which was strange for me.

My periods of coherence left them to debate whether I was really that bad, or if it was my medication.

In hindsight, Mom wishes that she would have thought more outside of the box, but she just kept going back to her depression episode and how she felt when she was sick. Sean's upset that he didn't trust his instincts and reach out more firmly to family for help. Mom's also angry that she just let life move on and wasn't always with me. She wishes that she would have stopped her life to pay more attention to me and not been so focused on my medication. She journaled on May 21: "Texted Sean & I am so worried about Jackie–she's getting worse."

Sean believes that by May 22 I had absolutely reached my lowest point and was on the verge of complete destruction. Thankfully, on that day, God led me to someone who saved my life.

CHAPTER 17

Sean and I went to my follow-up appointment at 11:00 a.m., on May 22. The appointment was with Nurse Practitioner Stephanie McDonald. I don't remember anything about that morning. Sean only remembers that he dressed me and helped me get ready, just like a child. Lacie came to our house to take care of the kids while we attended the appointment. I have no recollection of seeing Lacie or my kids before my appointment.

My memory of the encounter is of my sitting on the chair in her office and a little bit of soft light from a lamp. Sean sat adjacent to me on a loveseat. I can just barely see myself sitting there in the soft light, facing a woman behind a desk. Sean was somewhat close to me, talking to her. This was one of the first appointments where Sean was with me and was mostly talking with the provider about me and over me, while I just sat there. Had I remained my usual self, I would have hated it; but the reality was, I was nearly incapacitated, so not only was I not angry about what was happening, I really didn't even get it.

Sean was distraught that morning. He had been waiting for the appointment ever since I left the psychiatric ward, because he had watched me continuously decline and saw my behavior grow even more bizarre. In Sean's opinion, it hardly even took Stephanie moments to realize that something was seriously wrong with me and that it was not a behavioral issue.

Her notes state that prior to our appointment she had reviewed my chart, hospitalization records, discharge diagnosis, and medication. She included that the providers at the psychiatric ward saw my tremulous nature, fast rate of speech, and struggles with concentration and focus, which she was then able to personally verify.

Sean gave her nearly all of my information. He recalls that I tried to participate and answer some questions, but I was confused and a little agitated. He states that my impaired cognitive skills were readily apparent.

Sean told her that he was very concerned about me. My tremors and anxiety had seriously progressed to the point of being debilitating. He told her I was very physically active before, but I could no longer walk around the block. Nor could I even fix and style my daughter's hair anymore. He told her I was struggling to write, read, and type when I used to be a busy attorney. He reported that my concentration was poor, that I startled very easily, and that my comprehension was poor. He said that even with my concentrated effort, I could not stop my shaking and that it was waking me up at night. To get to the appointment, I had to hold Sean's arm or hand to walk with him, as I could barely walk on my own.

What I was able to convey to her that day was that I was "not sleeping" and had issues with sleep since the prior November. I described myself as having "perfectionist" tendencies and told her about my increased work stressors after starting my law firm. I also verified that Sean was a good support system for me. Sean states that past that, I didn't convey much of value to her. He said I tried to respond to what she asked me but was hyperactive about asking her for more mental health-type exercises to work on.

I continuously wrenched my hands together in front of her too. Leading up to that appointment and growing worse in severity after, I grew very fidgety, especially with my hands. I used the fingertips of one hand to pull back over the fingernails of the other hand and rotated pulling at my fingernails on each hand. I don't think I started those movements until I had been released from the psychiatric ward.

I remember doing it. It became obsessive and uncontrollable. I was experiencing dystonic movements, which are common in patients suffering with autoimmune encephalitis.

Stephanie noted my tremors and loss of muscle strength and endurance. I was dressed casually, had good eye contact, was cooperative, and sat upright in my chair, but I appeared fatigued. I had a slow gait, and Sean held my hand while I walked. My speech was clear, but I had some difficulty with linear thoughts. My mood was dysphoric. My attention was distracted but was easily redirected. My affect was blunted, and I was noted to be irritable at times, but not at her. Sean said that a few times I very angrily said, "This needs to end!"

I attempted to answer a depression screening before the appointment. Sean tried to ask me the questions and allow me to answer, and he filled in what I answered. He could see that I didn't understand what he was asking me. So rather than try to complete it for her, he wanted her to be able to ask me the questions so she could see how I struggled to respond. I responded with higher intensity that I had little interest or pleasure in doing things, that I had trouble concentrating, and that I was more fidgety or restless than usual. I responded with more nominal intensity that I had trouble sleeping and that I felt tired. My depression severity score that day was "moderate."

Stephanie immediately jumped into action and worked to get me a priority referral to neurology. The Bismarck and Fargo Sanford Neurologists were booked until September and October, but she very clearly articulated that I could not wait that long to be seen. She then called Mid Dakota Clinic to see if Neurologist Dr. Ralph Dunnigan could see me any sooner.

I remember her using the phone in front of us, and Sean crying. When she said "neurological," it vaguely registered with me that this could have something to do with my brain, but it didn't faze me, scare me, or bother me. I just sat there. Even though I could see and feel Sean crying and acting erratically, I just couldn't comprehend or process why. I no longer had the ability to comprehend and react to situations around me.

Sean left her office knowing that she was trying to get me into a neurologist and that he would await hearing from her later that day. She set a follow-up appointment with her in two weeks and directed Sean to take me to the ER if acute or continued concerns arose. I have no memory of leaving her office, only of Sean crying on the phone as we drove south.

What ensued after that appointment for everyone but me was sheer panic. Sean completely lost it in Stephanie's office and after. He called Mom, crying while driving, and told her Stephanie believed I had a neurological condition. Mom instantly panicked, dropped everything she was doing, and called Dad to tell him that they needed to get to Bismarck immediately. Mom's thoughts were very focused on one thing—a brain tumor. Sean began Googling neurological conditions, trying desperately to figure out what it was I had, based upon my symptoms. The Google results didn't paint any rosy pictures for him. He was terrified.

* * *

When we got back to our house, I remember barely making it to my lawn chair on the deck and plopping down. I can just barely see Lacie pushing my kids and her daughter on the swing, and they're all playing. Then I can see Sean talking to Lacie and bawling by the swing set, but I just sat there. I don't remember Lacie's reaction or anything else.

The next memory I have is of Mom and Sean talking to me about seeing a neurologist and my asking them questions while I'm still sitting in my chair on the deck, which would have been a few hours later.

Mom and Dad hustled to Bismarck to get to our house, and Sean's family immediately made arrangements to come too. Sean called Mike to inform him of the latest news and my rapidly changing diagnosis.

I was confused about the situation and repeatedly asked Mom and Sean, "What are we doing?" They kept trying to assure me that Stephanie was working to get me into a neurologist very soon because no one at Sanford could see me for months. They explained that we were waiting for her to call us back to see if she could get us an appointment. They didn't try to explain to me why I needed a neurologist, because they knew it was lost on me. As long as they could tell me what we were doing and where we were going, I was okay with the answer and was compliant. I had lost all agency since begging to be checked into the psychiatric ward.

By the end of the day, both Stephanie and Dr. Dunnigan's office confirmed that I had an appointment with him the next morning. Sean and my family were very happy that I was able to be seen so soon, but they were terrified about what they were going to learn, and they braced for a devastating diagnosis.

Everyone around me went into crisis mode. Everyone. My family rallied in hopes that I was not going to die, and the law firm rallied to prepare for my long-term absence. The visual for this part of my story is miles of dominos falling down one by one. My illness was taking down everyone around me in ways that I'll never know. My husband, my children, my parents, my extended family, my friends, my law firm, my clients, the firm's other clients, my future plans, my family's plans—nothing went unaffected.

The only person who was unfazed by the complete destruction of the present and future was me.

CHAPTER 18

The three days and four nights that followed our appointment with Stephanie were no more glamourous for me, and no less worrisome for my family. I was at a breaking point.

I was fatigued all day. My abilities and cognition remained on and off. I would speak a little and respond or just stare. I repeated to my family, "I feel like an empty shell." And along with the green that I had earlier seen on my phone, Mom reports that I kept talking about the color purple and how things "looked purple."

During the evenings, I barely spoke and went to bed very early, at around 6:30 or 7:00 p.m., to begin my thrashing and yelling. And at some point, I added something else into my nighttime arsenal—seizures.

I remember telling Mom and Sean that I was having seizures at night, in my bed. I have no idea how I knew this, as I had never before had a seizure, and I have never witnessed someone seizing. But I knew I was having them. I said, "It feels like lightning is going off in my head." I have slight memories of how my head felt when I believed it was happening. It was like having a light show in my head and explosions going off in my brain. I only remember accompanying physical effects on the morning of the 23rd.

I went upstairs to the kids' bathroom, and I think I had the intention of going to the bathroom, but I'm not sure. All I remember is that when I got close to the toilet, my arms and upper body started wildly flailing. The movement reverberated through my body, and I pooped all over. I yelled for Mom and she came up to help me. I remember that she had to almost lift me to get me into the bathtub, and she had to help me stand up to clean me off, because I was so shaky and weak. I felt terribly embarrassed and ashamed… and I cried. I was just competent enough to realize what was being taken from me, and I felt destroyed.

Mom and Sean remember my telling them about the seizures. They believed what I was telling them about how my head felt, but all they saw was my already confused, impaired, and uncoordinated state, and they figured that was to blame. I was the only witness, and an unreliable one at that.

May 23-Neurology Day 1

Sean and Mom accompanied me to my appointment with Dr. Dunnigan that morning. Our five-year-old daughter was at summer preschool, but our son, who was only three years old, came along with us. Mom and Sean prepared him to be very quiet during the appointment and told him not to talk when the doctor was talking.

I do have quite a bit of recollection from my appointment that first day. Yet my memory is nearly non-existent for the next two days.

When Dr. Dunnigan came into the room, something inside me told me that I had seen him before, and it was through work. It was a fleeting thought, but I knew I remembered him. I couldn't vocalize it, but I was correct. I had sat in on a deposition of Dr. Dunnigan, who was an expert witness in a case I worked on as a young lawyer.

I remember that I sat in the chair next to his chair, and Mom and Sean sat to my left. He first took in my medical history and recent events. Sean answered most of his questions and presented a lot of the background information, and that actually annoyed me a little. I wasn't as open to him speaking for me that day. In his notes, Dr. Dunnigan noted that I interjected quite a bit with the discussion and occasionally interrupted. My son also scolded me once while I was talking and said, "Mom, shh, don't talk, the doctor is talking." I don't know if I even heard it, and I didn't remember that he said it.

In Sean's opinion, Dr. Dunnigan could instantly see how out of it I was. Sean said I could answer a few questions, at best, but Sean had to do the bulk of the work to present my information. Even through my resistance, Sean did an amazing job of keeping our lives together and was doing everything he needed to do to get me a diagnosis.

Dr. Dunnigan described me as a "34-year-old active athletic right-handed woman who was well until 4:00 a.m. one day in November." Sean reported that, at first, the medication helped me sleep, and I reported that I became "more zoned during the day." I reported being burned out at work and that I had recently started a law firm with a partner. Sean corroborated everything and talked about the stressors I faced in 2017.

Sean stated that I was shaking, felt numbness in my arms, couldn't write, couldn't comprehend basic things, was forgetful, was confused, and he shared the story of my texting Lacie to tell her I had just seen her, when I hadn't. He said that I twitched, rubbed my hands together, and that my memory was really off and on.

I reported that I had chronic ringing in my ears for four weeks and that I had a very tight chest. I told the doctor that many times I didn't know whether I was having a panic attack or a heart attack. In describing my athleticism, I told him, "I ran my legs till I broke them both."

I said, "I'm so dizzy right now, I don't know how to function." I reported that I was sleeping a little better, but was "in and out a lot," and that I felt like I abruptly woke up a lot. I said, "I feel like someone has strung me out on drugs for the longest time."

I reported that I didn't remember my dreams and didn't think I dreamt much. I only remembered the one dream where the man opposite me in the divorce "shot me." Sean verified that I was fidgety and talked a lot in my sleep, and I thrashed and shook at night.

I managed to tell Dr. Dunnigan about my colitis, and Mom and Sean recall that raising a red flag to him. I stated that my colitis had recently stopped. I told him about losing control of my bowels that morning and stated that, "I had a little seizure." Even though my colitis had been the bane of my existence leading up to my illness, it was probably life saving for me to talk about it that day, as Dr. Dunnigan drew the correlation from that condition to another autoimmune disorder.

My first neurological examination was performed by Dr. Dunnigan, and Sean and Mom remained present with me in the room. At the beginning of the test, I sat on the examination table, and he told me to close my eyes. Just as he was coming toward me, I opened them, and he frightened me. Sean said I looked terrified, and I remember Dr. Dunnigan apologized for scaring me.

My speech was fluent, although it was pressured. I was a little tangential but tried to stay on task. I sat relatively comfortably in the examination room but was a little fidgety. I struggled to know left from right and had some difficulty with comprehension.

I remember him pushing up and down on my toes and asking me if they were positioned up or down. I thought it was very hard, and Sean said nearly all of my answers were wrong. Dr. Dunnigan noted that I struggled significantly with the task. I was not able to comprehend what he wrote on my hand with his finger, purely by the sensation of touch. When he placed a key in my right hand, I fiddled with it for quite a while and concluded that it was a butterfly, but I did recognize a safety pin in my left hand.

My muscle strength was intact, but I performed poorly on heel-to-shin testing. I struggled to run my right heel over my left shin and vice versa. I walked fairly steady for him, but I could not walk with my eyes closed, as I was too dizzy. When I was asked to do a test where I had to stand upright and hold my arms out straight in front of me, with my palms up and my eyes closed, I was very unsettled and kept falling backward. Everyone was afraid I was going to fall over, including me.

My second neurological examination was the Montreal Cognitive Assessment. Sean and Mom couldn't stay with me, so they left for the waiting room with our son asleep in Sean's arms.

I don't remember much at the beginning, just that Dr. Dunnigan's nurse, Kelsie, was with me, and there was another lady. Kelsie gave me the directions for the first part of the test and asked me to complete it a few times. I bawled the entire time, and I remember looking at her through the tears saying, "I don't know what you're asking me to do." I felt like Kelsie and the other lady just looked at one another with wide eyes. We moved on from that part, and I drew a cube. I was shaky, but I could do it. Then she asked me to draw a clock. I'm not sure what went on in my head, although I think I knew that I couldn't do it. I attempted it, but at some point I just gave up and left it how I had it. She then asked me to recall and repeat words she gave me, to name animals, and to count.

When Mom and Sean returned, I was waiting there with Dr. Dunnigan, and I told them that the test was "awful." I vividly remember that while we were all sitting there, Dr. Dunnigan looked at Mom and Sean and said, "Well, her clock is interesting," and he handed them a copy of the paper I had drawn on. Mom saw the clock and felt an instant sickness inside of her. I just sat there. I heard him say it, and I knew I was a mess, but I didn't say anything.

I performed poorly on the test and scored an 18 out of 30. A score of 26 and above is normal. A score of 18-25 shows mild cognitive impairment. My clock really *is* "interesting." I was supposed to draw a clock at ten minutes past eleven. I drew the circle and had the twelve in the correct position. I then clustered 1-2-3-4-5-6-7-8 all down the right side of the circle. My 8 was about where the 6 should have been. I could not draw the left side at all, even with multiple attempts. When I gave up, I just put down a 9 about where the 8 should go. Basically, the entire left side of the clock is blank, and there are no hands on the clock.

Dr. Dunnigan then asked Mom and Sean if they had ever read the book *Brain on Fire*. Neither one of them had heard of the book and questioned how a book was relevant to me. He said it was a good book and that it was very relevant to me because he was quite sure that I had the author's (Susannah Cahalan) rare brain illness, autoimmune encephalitis. He shared with them that she wrote the book about her experience with the disease. Her immune system mistakenly attacked her brain and caused it to be inflamed, which resulted in her experiencing strange behavior and possessing symptoms similar to mine.

Sean and Mom immediately began asking questions about possible recovery. "Will Jackie recover? Did that woman return to normal?" He answered that she fully recovered and that most people are also able to recover, which was good news. Mom and Sean started to breathe big sighs of relief, but still felt distressed as Dr. Dunnigan left open the possibility of other medical and mental health diagnoses and ordered further testing. He also didn't totally rule out that my stress and sleep deprivation were the cause of all my issues, but he believed my problems had escalated despite the fact that I seemed to be getting some sleep.

I was assessed as having acute confusion, colitis, insomnia, and impaired cognition. He wanted to exclude other structural diseases and evaluate me for Lyme disease, heavy metals, and autoimmune encephalitis. He also wanted to check me for Wilson's disease, Whipple's disease, porphyria, and some others. He ordered an MRI of my brain, an EEG, and the Mayo Clinic's autoimmune encephalitis blood work.

I also vividly remember at the end of the visit how Dr. Dunnigan asked Sean and Mom, as I sat right there, "You don't leave her alone, do you?" They both emphatically answered, "No." And again, I just sat there and stared through it all. I heard it and I kind of understood it, but I couldn't do much with it. I was a thirty-four-year-old mother of two and a successful trial lawyer who couldn't be left alone.

Mom and Sean already told him that I wasn't driving, but he reiterated that I clearly could not do so. He also recommended that my family continue to supervise me twenty-four hours a day. He knew the workup was going to take several days, and on the date of our first appointment it was the Wednesday before Memorial Day weekend. Thus, he was cognizant of the long weekend slowing down the process. He told Sean that if I worsened over the long weekend, he should take me to St. Mary's Hospital in Rochester, Minnesota, for an urgent evaluation and likely admittance.

Dr. Dunnigan spent eighty minutes with us that day. His brilliance and dedication were life saving for me, just like Stephanie's were the day before. Without their quick thinking and actions, I believe I would have suffered permanent brain damage or, even worse, death.

The first appointment with Dr. Dunnigan went well, and my family started to have glimpses of answers, but it was only the beginning. They had to do some online research to try to figure out just what exactly autoimmune encephalitis was. And I had to go to the lab for blood work before we could leave.

Two of the last photographs of me were taken on May 7, where I'm with my daughter at her kindergarten open house, and on May 8, where I'm outside with my son for a walk, after I left work. In spite of how I felt, I looked perfectly normal in each photograph. There is another photograph that Sean took of me and my daughter on May 19. It's of me sitting in my recliner in my pajamas, with my afghan on my legs, and I'm kissing my daughter. I look very tired in that photograph, and my eyes are sunken in.

The last photograph of me is at my blood draw after my appointment with Dr. Dunnigan. I was wearing a favorite old, gray University of North Dakota T-shirt and blue hiking shorts. While I was sick and doctoring, and Sean helped me get ready, he said I mostly chose casual athletic clothes to dress in. I was always able to put my own hair up in a messy ponytail, which was routine for me. Mom put a necklace on me that day. It was one that I frequently wore, and it had both my kids' birthstones in it. I only know what I was wearing that day, and how I looked in my darkest of days, because of that one photo. It appears to be me, but if you look closely, I'm tired, and there's not a lot behind my eyes. I'm looking up smiling, with my hands in my lap, but it's not really me looking back at the camera.

Mom journaled: "Jackie saw Dr. Dunnigan at Mid Dakota. Spent 2 ½ hours with her. She flunked memory test. Rough day & nights. Scared of tumor. Slept poorly–Jackie talks in her sleep."

May 24-Neurology Day 2

I have virtually no recollection of my May 24 appointments. I know I had an MRI that day, but I don't remember anything about it. I only have one slight memory from seeing Dr. Dunnigan after the MRI.

The MRI of my brain was in the morning, and Sean and Mom accompanied me. They stayed in the waiting room during the scan. With all the doctoring I had done in the past for my shoulder, legs, and sinus infections, I was no stranger to MRIs or CT scans. However, I had never before been placed in a small, confined tube with an active brain illness and tremors.

When I got done, I reported to Mom and Sean that I kept hitting the button they gave me in the event I needed out of the MRI. Per Sean, the way I explained it was almost like I was a drunk, giggling girl, saying, "I just kept hitting it." But I was not giggling, I was serious, and I couldn't explain why I kept doing it. I'm sure they told me to lie very still, because they do that at the beginning of every scan, but it was impossible for me to comply because I couldn't stop shaking. It was involuntary and severe.

I'm not sure if it was during the test or after, but they discussed completely putting me under and redoing the scan so they could get a better image. The image they obtained that day was of poor quality because I shook so badly.

We met with Dr. Dunnigan after the MRI, and the only memory I have of the day is him saying to Mom and Sean, "Her brain looks good." Sean and Mom cheered with relief, and I think they both cried and hugged Dr. Dunnigan. I could feel their relief and what a big deal it was, but I just sat there. Something told me that my brain looking good was good news, but it didn't register too much. Mom was already telling people, "Thank God she doesn't understand how serious this is." The usual Jackie would have been a nervous wreck that she possibly had a brain tumor or an abnormality in her brain. But reality had no meaning to sick Jackie.

Dr. Dunnigan stated that I was alert, pleasant, and similar to how I was the day before. I still lacked some insight. I struggled somewhat to communicate, and my speech was deliberate, but I was appropriate. I could get up and walk steadily.

He reported that I still needed to undergo an EEG, but that it hadn't yet been set up. All the lab work from the day before, including the autoimmune encephalitis panel, had already been sent off to the Mayo Clinic for testing. Considering all the facts we had in front of us, and because the MRI showed no abnormalities of my brain, Dr. Dunnigan and my family agreed to have me go forward with a spinal tap to look for any irregularities and to determine whether I had any antibodies that are known to be present with autoimmune encephalitis. Dr. Dunnigan wanted the spinal tap to be done quickly so they could continue to gather all the relevant and necessary data as soon as possible.

Sean's older sister, Shelly, arrived from out of town after my appointments that day, and his mother, Kathy, was already at our house. I have no real memories of my family and Sean's family all staying in our house. I also don't remember hugging anyone during this time. Sean assures me that I continued to give my children affection when I could, but because I didn't tolerate much no one was too affectionate with me. However, while I was sitting at the table that afternoon, either Kathy or Shelly walked by and put her arm on my shoulder in an act of compassion. I can't remember who did it, yet I know that her touch transcended my inability to comprehend. It's the only touch I can remember during that time, and I distinctly recall how it made me feel. It told me something was wrong with me and that my family was worried. Yet I continued to just sit there and stare, almost completely defeated in all of my abilities, even though that touch registered with me.

That evening, my family allowed me to do something that in hindsight they wish they had not. My daughter had an end of the year picnic for her preschool at a local park in town. I had taken the kids the year before, and we had fun. Apparently, I was adamant that I would attend the picnic, despite my state. Sean and Mom kindly tried to talk me out of it, but I was determined to be there for my daughter. Sean, Mom, the kids, and I all went to the park, and it didn't go very well. I do have a few memories of being there.

All the food was in the picnic shelter, and I tried to help my daughter get her plate. I remember I struggled terribly to stand in line and to even try to help her get her food or hold a plate. The weakness in my legs and knees almost collapsed me, and I felt like every kid there was going to knock me over. I then recall sitting on the grass with my family, and a long way away from me I could see my friend Chanda and her mom and son eating. I don't remember if I even waved at her. I was incapable of doing anything basic. My daughter acted out, because I couldn't help her, and she sensed something was wrong with me by the way I looked and acted. I had become weird and scary.

Our time there was short lived. I remember trying to walk to the car, and I had to hold Mom's arm. I knew people were staring at me, but it didn't really bother me. Yet, before we went to the picnic, I apparently ordered Sean and Mom to not let anyone speak to me.

Per Sean, my daughter's teacher tried to speak to me before we left, and I ignored her. He claims it was obvious I wasn't myself, and people noticed. Outside of my medical appointments, I hadn't been out in public at all since I had left work weeks prior to that, and, truly, I had no business being outside of the house in my condition.

The next day, the teacher wrote me a message on Facebook that I didn't see for months: "So sorry I didn't get to visit with you at all last night. Been thinking of you all day today for some reason. Was everything ok last night?"

* * *

That day was just like many others before. Some of the family took care of the kids, some accompanied me to appointments, and when we weren't in appointments, we all just hung around our home. But that night in particular, the atmosphere was more somber. They all sat together and cried on and off after I went to bed. They were scared to death. Any sight of my children overwhelmed everyone with emotion. All they could think of was what the illness was doing to my mind and spirit, and what if it took my life and took me from my children?

Sean stayed in touch with Lacie to keep her informed, and he also communicated with Mike. Ashley and Betsy were still trying to help both Mike and Sean as much as they could. Apparently, I repeatedly told my family, "The law firm is fine." I assured them, "It's in good hands." I continually said there was nothing to worry about because I was blissfully away from it all. Mike and the staff didn't feel like everything was "fine." They were operating in their own day-to-day crisis mode, and they questioned whether I would ever return.

Mom journaled: "Jackie had MRI of brain. Saw Dr. Dunnigan after and he said her brain is good. He is thinking she might have AE."

I quietly hung out with everyone that day. And that night, I slept diagonally in bed and talked loudly, while visions of purple probably danced in my head.

May 25-Neurology Day 3

May 25 was the Friday before Memorial Day weekend, and I had my spinal tap early that morning. A guy that I knew of, named Chris, was the man who drew my blood before the procedure. He dated a friend of mine from Bowman, named Rachel. I had never met him, but had seen him in pictures with Rachel, so I recognized him. When I was in my room later, lying down on the table, Rachel came in to discuss my anesthesia with me. I knew that Rachel was a nurse practitioner at the hospital and administered anesthesia. I recognized her, and Sean says I carried on some conversation with her.

I was ahead of Rachel in high school, but we played basketball together. Rachel was notoriously flighty back then. However, I had gotten to know Rachel more personally over the past few years, and I was impressed at how mature and wise she was. I had also heard from others that she was an exceptional nurse. When she told me she would be administering my anesthesia, I was nervous for a split second, because I thought about Rachel from high school. But I quickly got over it and trusted that she would do well by me. That is all I remember from the dreaded spinal tap.

After the procedure was done, we went home. I was told to lie on my back for most of the day to make sure the puncture didn't bleed and to help avoid a headache. I don't remember any specific ways to describe the pain, except that it was unbearable. I have only a slight memory of being on the futon, but it hurt to lie down, and it hurt to sit up. Apparently, it was a long day for me.

Sean and Mom report that I was in a great deal of pain. I had a terrible headache and nothing relieved it, but I was fairly coherent that day. Mom journaled: "Jackie had a spinal tap. Got a bad headache so supposed to lie on back. It was a nice warm day so I lied in the hammock & she on beach towel on lawn."

For a few days, I only asked to eat sweets, which was very atypical of me. I asked Shelly to make me Bananas Foster. I have no idea why I wanted that, because I had never before eaten it, but it was stuck in my head. She was going to make it for me after my spinal tap, but I was so sick I didn't even want it. She then left that evening.

I went to bed at 6:30 p.m. that night, which was even earlier than usual. I'm sure it was in part because of all the pain I was in, but also because my body was telling me to try to rest a little while I could… because the worst was yet to come. All of the neurons misfiring in my brain were finally going to put on a grand finale fireworks show, and I had to live through it.

CHAPTER 19

Earlier that evening, I ate a strawberry popsicle. A few hours later, I threw up all over myself in bed. I hollered out for Mom to come and help me. I only remember the moment as I sat up and looked at my red puke and felt like my head was splitting. Mom helped me clean up and got me some pink shorts to wear, since I had vomited on my pajama bottoms. The blue tie-dye pajamas I was wearing were my favorites, as Sean had gifted them to me many years prior. I think I went back to sleep for a while after that.

I remember the moment it hit. It was like the physical feeling of lightning striking me and an earthquake ripping through me all at once. It had an instantaneous feeling of terror and destruction. The explosion started in my brain and reverberated through my entire body. It caught and spread like wildfire.

It is my memory that I sat upright in bed when it felt like the lightning bolt struck my head. My hands and arms immediately started to fly wildly and uncontrollably all over the place, as if I was trying to brace myself while the earthquake tore through me. For just a second, I wanted to scream out for help, but I couldn't. I peed my pants. And after that, it all goes black.

The memory I have is only an instant long, but I can still feel the desire to scream. I can feel my arms moving so rapidly and uncontrollably that they are almost screaming out too. It is the worst of all the nightmares, all the terrors, and all the episodes I had in that bed for those seven months, in a few split seconds.

* * *

Sean was next door, sleeping in our son's room, when he heard me. Mom was sleeping on the futon on the main floor, and she heard me just as Sean did. As Sean entered our room, Mom was running up the stairs behind him. The sounds they were hearing were the sounds of a violent seizure. Mom knew that I was having a seizure even before she could see me. She claims that there is no mistaking that sound and that she would recognize it anywhere. She refers to the sound as "guttural," as in deep in the throat or gullet. They both could also hear my breathing, which was heavy, labored, and loud. Mom describes it as deep and scary, like a person is gasping. By the sounds of my breathing, she also feared that I had aspirated.

Sean instantly observed my legs flying around uncontrollably under the blanket. I was lying on my right side, with all my weight on my right shoulder, under my blanket, in the fetal position. My mouth was open, my eyes were rolled into the back of my head, and I was making dreadful sounds. Mom jumped into bed with me, to try to keep me from falling out, and started talking to me, but I was unconscious. By my tonic-clonic movements, my loss of control, my loss of function, and because I was unconscious, Mom knew I was having a grand mal seizure.

Sean quickly called 911 and paced back and forth in our bedroom while talking to the dispatcher. When he called, it was about 3:00 a.m. in the early morning hours of Saturday, May 26. The dispatcher asked Sean to allow her to hear how I was breathing, but then she realized that she could hear my labored breathing through the phone. She told Sean to turn on the porch lights at our home and have the door open for the first responders. Kathy awoke with the commotion and waited for them at the front door.

Within about fifteen minutes, four Bismarck firemen arrived at our home. Captain Matt Wilke took my vitals and asked whether I had been drinking, used any illicit drugs, and whether I had ever had a seizure before. Sean told him that he believed I had autoimmune encephalitis, and Captain Wilke had never before heard of it. At about that same time, I started to regain consciousness and began speaking in word salad as I came to. Sean and Mom report that my eyes grew very large with fright at all the men standing in my bedroom, and that I looked and acted very scared.

The firemen got their board to transport me to the ambulance. When they first started to move me, I held my right arm in pain, and as they strapped me onto the board I yelled, "Ow!" Everyone was puzzled as to why but just kept going. Just as they were getting ready to take me out on the board, two paramedics came into our room, and Captain Wilke gave them my vitals. Since I was breathing and my heart was working, the EMTs didn't need to hook me up to any machines, but they wanted to get me to the hospital quickly.

Sean was happy that the firemen were the first to respond, as they were very calm and strong enough to transport me down our steep staircase on the board. As they took me down the stairs, I was just barely conscious, but I continued to loudly yell out in pain.

Right outside our front door in the middle of the dark street sat a forty ton, red fire truck with flashing lights, and a lit up ambulance had backed up to the sidewalk. The firemen transported me from their board to the paramedics' board in our front yard, and I was loaded into the back of the ambulance. I'll never get to view the scene, though, because it was accidentally erased from our home security system. And by the time I asked for Sean's 911 call, it no longer existed.

While I was loaded into the ambulance and Sean was told he could ride with, Mom asked the firemen if they would give her a ride to the hospital. She raced back into the house in her pajamas, got dressed, and hopped in the fire truck with the firemen, and they drove her to the hospital. Kathy stayed at the house with our kids, who were thought to be asleep.

As I rode in the ambulance, I was confused and scared. I was still in and out of consciousness and struggled to speak clearly. A few times, I asked Sean where I was going and asked him where he was. After he would answer, I would respond, "okay," and then I would pass out.

Sean asked the paramedics to take me to CHI/St. Alexius hospital, where I had given birth to our two children. They drove right into the emergency garage, and the head nurse who had taken care of me met them there. I was taken straight into the ER, and Sean was able to stay with me. Dr. Abe Storms was my attending ER physician that night.

Unlike when Sean and Ashley had taken me to the Sanford ER a few weeks prior, the ER was not quiet that Saturday morning. Sean heard about two drug overdoses, law enforcement officers were hanging around the halls, and he could hear someone's stomach getting pumped. He also overheard someone walking around saying, "I don't exist." He was overwhelmed with panic, fear, hysteria, and the repeated question of *What the hell is happening to us?*

CHAPTER 20

My memory of the ER has three scenes. I can hear things going on around me, but I cannot see any people, colors, or faces… only bright light.

The first scene: There are people in the room talking to me, jabbing needles in me, and all I can see are the bright lights above me. As I come to, there's a woman in my right ear telling me, "You've had a seizure, and your shoulder is dislocated and broken." Notwithstanding my state, the word seizure penetrated my numb mind. It scared me, and I was almost baffled, as never before did I think I would hear those words. I remember thinking *holy shit!*

The next scene: I again come to, and more attendants are in my room. They're telling me that they have to put my shoulder back in place. They're fiddling around with my pajama tank top, and someone finally asks me if she can cut it off. I respond affirmatively, and then I proceed to tell her that Sean gave me those pajamas as a gift, coincidentally, after I had shoulder surgery. Then I feel someone jab me in the left arm, and it's lights out for me.

The final scene: I come to as they're placing the immobilizer brace around my waist and wrist to hold my shoulder in place. I can hear the Velcro ripping. I feel another stab in my arm, and I know it's potent because I'm knocked out again, and this time for quite a while.

The next two memories I have are of two physicians speaking to me. I believed that the encounters happened in the ER, but they didn't happen until later in the day when I was in my hospital room.

The first memory I have is a little more vivid, as I can see his face and hear his voice. I am seeing Dr. Troy Pierce, the on-call orthopedic surgeon. Since I moved to Bismarck, I had heard of Dr. Pierce because not only is he a surgeon in town, but we are distant cousins, and he is also from Bowman. I had never before met him but had seen pictures of him. When he showed up in my room and spoke to me, I instantly knew it was him. All I remember him saying is, "You did serious damage to your shoulder," and I can see him standing in the doorway in his white lab coat. That's the only memory I have of him in my room.

The second memory is of Dr. Shiraz Hyder, a neurologist at the hospital, who cared for me during my stay. I feel like he and Mom are standing directly over me, and they are talking. Mom is very concerned about my being transported to Mayo and is almost pleading with him. I can hear her saying, "How can she get there? She can't travel." I remember Dr. Hyder telling her to just slow down and that they were going to work everything out. That conversation is pretty blurry, but my family informs me that it may be somewhat accurate because the discussion of the need for me to be transported to Mayo had started. I also remember Dr. Hyder telling me that I would lose my driver's license for six months because I had a seizure. In my head, I told myself that I had bigger fish to fry, so that didn't bother me at all.

* * *

Sean stayed with me in my ER room for about an hour until he went to the waiting room to get Mom, and then she was allowed to be in my room too. I was mostly unconscious for the first few hours. And if I was awake, I told them that my arm hurt or asked them questions about where I was.

Sean gave the usual information to Dr. Storms: No, she doesn't use drugs. We think she has autoimmune encephalitis. This time, Sean had to also add that I didn't have a history of seizures. Sean was deathly afraid of what he had just witnessed and was terrified that I would have another one. Dr. Storms quickly prescribed me seizure medication. And, based upon my complaint that my arm hurt, he ordered an x-ray of my right arm.

The results showed that not only was my shoulder dislocated, it was also broken. My right humeral head was fractured. In Sean's opinion, Dr. Storms' expression was incredulous when he told them. He asked whether I fell out of bed, and both Mom and Sean denied that I could have done so, as I was having the seizure in my bed when they found me. They both doubted that I could have fallen out of bed and then got back into bed in the fetal position that they found me in while seizing. Sean and Mom were also a little surprised, but not completely dumbfounded because of the chronic problems I had with my right shoulder over the years. Sean began feeling paranoid after all the questions and looks of surprise. He worried that people were questioning whether he had abused me.

Dr. Storms asked Mom and Sean for consent to reposition my shoulder and then asked them to leave the room. He made it clear that they would not want to witness or hear the repositioning, which I can attest to. The pain and bizarre feeling of your shoulder hanging out of its socket, and the idea of the noise it makes when it goes back in, makes you want to puke. Sean and Mom left the room and tried to sleep. I was given propofol at 6:25 a.m., and my shoulder was repositioned in the ER. I was out of my anesthesia by 6:45 a.m. and given morphine for my pain. Sean and Mom were allowed back in my room not too long after the procedure was complete, and I was placed in my immobilizer brace.

At about 8:00 a.m., Dr. Vivek Vadehra came down to the ER to meet with Sean and Mom and admit me to the hospital. Sean and Mom gave Dr. Vadehra the same recitations about my health and history. Given my fragile condition and the fear that I would have another seizure, Dr. Vadehra wanted me placed near a nurses station. At about 10:00 a.m., I was moved to my room on the oncology floor, as it was the only floor in the hospital that had an open room next to the nurses. From there, my family endured the next phase of my care—the hospital stay.

CHAPTER 21

May 26–Hospital Day 1

The next five days continued the all-hands-on-deck crisis mentality that my family had been acting under for the past four days. At home that early Saturday morning, Kathy took care of the kids, and my Aunt Nicole, who lives nearby, came over to our house to also help out.

When my aunt arrived at our house, she found the kids doing very well with Kathy. She took them outside to play on the swing set and tried to talk to them a little bit about the last night's events. She told them that an ambulance had come to get me in the night and that I went to the hospital. Whether she truly knew or not, and what all she was comprehending at five years old, we will never know, but my daughter responded, "I know," and left it at that. We believe she heard all the men coming up and down the stairs and me yelling out in pain, and either looked out of her room or out her window. In all the chaos, neither Sean, Mom, nor Captain Wilke saw her come out of her room, but she's a light sleeper, and it was a lot of commotion.

Sean and Mom made themselves comfortable in my hospital room and waited for the specialists to come in. Dr. Pierce was the first specialist to visit, and that's where I have my memory of him. His opinion was that my shoulder fracture and dislocation were the direct result of my grand mal seizure and that because of the serious damage done I would probably need surgery. Mom states that she was in complete disbelief at the idea of shoulder surgery on top of my already full medical plate.

Shortly thereafter, Dr. Hyder came to my room and began a thorough assessment. He was able to get a lot of the necessary medical information from talking to Mom and Sean and from the records he could access on the electronic system.

During his examination, I was noted to be drowsy and unreliable, so he didn't do much cognitive testing on me. I was easily aroused, but kept falling asleep. I answered appropriately and could follow simple single-step commands. I answered the correct date, month, and year, and identified the hospital where I was staying. I could not count backward from one hundred by sevens. I could not subtract seven from ninety-three. I could not spell "world" backward, and I could not remember three out of four objects after five minutes.

Numerous times while Dr. Hyder was trying to examine me, including while shining a flashlight in my eyes, I fell asleep. Mom had to repeatedly yell my name to get me to wake up for him, which is only funny in hindsight.

Even with my right arm in the brace, I was able to squeeze Dr. Hyder's fingers strongly on both sides and move both arms well. I could also move my toes downward. He deferred my trying to walk, as I was confined to my bed at that time and had a catheter in. I was not allowed up and to walk until the second day.

He agreed that my diagnosis was likely autoimmune or paraneoplastic encephalitis and questioned whether I was too early in the disease to have an abnormal MRI or abnormal cerebral spinal fluid. He noted that my condition was rare and that it wasn't seen much in Bismarck. Upon his assessment and review of records, he strongly believed that I needed an expedited appointment at the Mayo Clinic in Rochester, Minnesota, for further evaluation and treatment. His recommendation of the Mayo Clinic started the next wave of panic and slight discord in my family—whether I needed to be immediately transported there.

As Dr. Vadehra was in the process of getting me stabilized and comfortable, and specialists came in and out of the room, Sean's phone started to blow up. The news that I was ill and in the hospital spread quickly and began a blast of social media, emails, texts, and phone calls. Sean did his best to respond, and Mom was also trying to notify the family of my status. Sean was consumed by the chaos and over-whelmed by all the questions.

By the end of the first day, Sean posted an update on Facebook. In his words, "I wanted to give as many people as I could as much information as possible." He received an outpouring of support and concern from friends and family and people unknown to us. People were blown away by what had transpired, because outside of a few friends and family, no one even knew that I was sick, much less did they know the enormity of what I had faced for the past few months. Upon hearing the news, people were afraid I was going to die, or worse yet, that I would live, but be an entirely different person.

Sean texted Mike with the news. Any hope for my coming back to the firm in the near future was dismantled. The only question on everyone's mind was whether we would use my long-term disability insurance or my life insurance.

May 27-30–Hospital Days 2-5

On May 27, Mom journaled: "Jackie's in a lot of pain with her shoulder. Getting IV morphine. Dr. Vadehra's nice."

On May 28, she journaled: "In hospital. Sean and I spend all day with her. Sean or Mike [my brother] brings the kids up. She quit shaking after seizure and rests much better at night."

It was to everyone's disbelief but was a welcomed sight. The seizure seemed to "reset" me. Right away, Mom and Sean noticed that I was shaking less and that I seemed to be more at ease when I rested during the day and at night.

Monday, May 28, Memorial Day, is the first day that I start to have some memories of my hospital room. The most vivid memory I have of that day is my family walking into my room. My little brother David was in the lead, and Dad and my older brother, Mike, walked in behind. It caught my attention when Mike walked in, since he lived out of state, and it really brightened my spirits. What I remember saying, almost rhetorically, was, "Mike's here?" I didn't know the whole story of how much it had put him and his family out for him to arrive in Bismarck, but I was very happy to see him along with the rest of my family.

Sean brought the kids to see me that day too. I only have a faint memory of them doing puzzles on the floor by my bed. When Sean asked our son to kiss me, he said, "No, I don't want to get sick."

I believe God took my memories of my kids during most of May and June, so I'll never have to remember what their faces looked like when they saw me ill and hospitalized.

By about the third day, I have more memories of Dr. Vadehra coming into my room, but I didn't like him there at all. I really enjoyed him and found him to be wonderfully comforting and kind, but he always asked me questions to test my brain, and I hated that. I knew what he was doing, and it frustrated me, because I knew I couldn't answer much of what he asked me. My mind was still absent, so basic questions were hard to answer, but there was still enough of my personality left to be upset when I knew I couldn't do it. Per Sean and Mom, I continuously struggled to pronounce "Vadehra," but he always reassured me that it was okay. I also stared at his name on the marker board in my room and often asked Mom and Sean how to say it.

One question I got a lot during the hospitalization was as follows. Q: Who is the current president? A: Donald Trump. Numerous times beginning in the psychiatric ward, I wanted to answer: Hillary Clinton. But I tried to always answer truthfully to prove that I lived in reality.

What I don't remember, but Mom does, is many times when people asked me questions. I looked at her for help and pleaded with my eyes for her to answer for me, but the doctors wouldn't allow it. I had to try to answer for myself, and it was miserable.

The pain in my shoulder was intense, so I was kept on morphine for quite a few days. And because I was so weak and unsteady, it took me days to get out of bed. The first time I remember getting out of bed, I was by myself, and I looked at myself in the mirror. I don't remember much of what I saw looking back at me, except that my earrings were in funny places. I had a third piercing in my left lobe that I hadn't had an earring in since high school. An earring was in that hole, but I didn't have an earring in my left cartilage, where I usually have one. I laughed a little to myself when I realized that Mom had repierced one of my ears. She took my earrings out for my MRI, because I wasn't coordinated enough to do so, and when she put them back in she didn't know where they all went.

I complained a lot about how my long hair looked because I didn't have the ability to pull it up without the use of both hands, and it had grown quite lengthy with the chaos of the prior months. It's never been Mom's forte to work with long hair, so she began mentioning to me that maybe I should think about cutting it shorter while my shoulder was immobilized.

* * *

Sean's panic for me, our family, our livelihood, well-being, finances, and everything possible, was immediate. He felt like all the competing demands placed him inside a tornado. He tried to weigh in with the law firm and my friends who were graciously operating there for me by proxy. He listened to my family's concerns and entertained all the generous offers for help from friends while he obsessed about the uncertainty of my short- and long-term needs and my prognosis. His gut feeling was that I was going to need serious help, and that Mom would need to take care of me. He quickly made up his mind that he would sell most of our assets and relocate us to Bowman, so he could work full-time and Mom could take care of me and the children upon her nearing retirement. Our home, camper, my car, Montessori preschool and endless activities for the children, my thriving law firm, the YMCA, restaurants we frequented, our friends, and everything we loved in Bismarck would be lost and replaced by a small-town lifestyle with few options for school, entertainment, and activity that both Sean and I never desired to return to. On top of all of this, the question of whether I should go to the Mayo Clinic and, if so, when, was looming.

From the date of my admission, and for a few days after, the question of whether I needed to be immediately transported to Rochester was thoroughly discussed and debated. Sean felt like my doctors and family leaned toward my going to Mayo immediately. He wasn't opposed to it, but he had many fears and concerns that he wanted to address before he could make a sound decision.

Sean worried about what was happening to my brain and what any further delay in treatment might do to me. I had already gone into neurological failure and had a grand mal seizure, so he was terrified of letting the disease go untreated, and he was more terrified that I was going to have another seizure. He didn't want me to get any worse. He felt like the doctors seemed to agree that I had autoimmune encephalitis, so he questioned why they couldn't just start treating me in Bismarck. When my brother Mike did some research on treatment options, he saw that autoimmune encephalitis could be treated with steroids, so Sean couldn't see why the doctors in Bismarck couldn't just start the steroids right away. One time, when Dr. Hyder asked about our treatment plans and discussed options in front of me, I spoke up to say that I wanted to stay in Bismarck and not leave my kids. Given my state, my opinion didn't carry a lot of weight with anyone.

Sean was also very fearful of anyone trying to transport me to Rochester, which was a nine-hour drive from Bismarck. He didn't believe I had the ability to ride that far in a car because I was already so fragile and broken. He was also afraid of my having another seizure during transport. Dr. Hyder also didn't believe I could travel, so he looked into having Mayo's private plane come to Bismarck to retrieve me, which scared Sean for many reasons. The thought of my being so sick that I would need to be airlifted to Mayo was overwhelming. He was also afraid that our family's financial future already hung by a thread, and he believed that the transport costs and medical costs were going to break us. And no matter how I got to Mayo, he wasn't clear about which clinic I would be sent to when I arrived. Since it was a holiday weekend, it was hard for my doctors to make substantial contact with Mayo, and that frightened him. He worried that, without a solid plan of where I was going once I got to Rochester, something bad would happen to me. It was very hard for him to process all the uncertainties and variables standing in the way of an immediate move to Mayo.

Mom believed that it was absolutely critical that I get to Mayo, but she was very worried about my traveling in my fragile state. She was worried about anyone outside of the Mayo Clinic trying to diagnose or treat me. She knew that Dr. Dunnigan's office had sent my labs to the Mayo Clinic, but with the holiday weekend everything was shut down between Dr. Dunnigan's office and the clinic. She felt like my providers at the hospital were stuck in the middle of nowhere, trying to help us form a plan.

Mom was very worried about all the outside pressure Sean faced between the law firm, our finances, and the medical decisions he was being asked to make. She wanted him to slow down and only focus on my health. Everyone around him agreed, as they hated to see him concerned with anything outside of the immediate demands of my health. Both of our families told him they would help us out, so they could hopefully put his mind at ease about our finances and a possible relocation. Per Sean, he never felt at ease about anything.

What finally solidified Sean's comfort level with my staying in Bismarck and not trying to rush to Mayo, was that the seizure medication was effective. My competence and alertness also got a bit better with each day, and my shaking drastically reduced. I started to look and sound like less of a ticking time bomb than I was before, and that helped ease everyone's mind.

* * *

We did have a few laughs as I was stuck in my bed for nearly five days, and my family was stuck there with me. During a time when all of my family was in my room, including my younger brother David, I was asking a lot of questions. I needed constant reassurance, so it was common for me to ask about my status, and I usually repeated my questions.

I asked if the ambulance came to my house after I had the seizure, and my family said, "Yes." I next asked if the ambulance went to the hospital after, and my family said, "Yes." I then genuinely asked, "Did I ride with?" David restrained himself from saying, *No Jackie, you drove the firetruck*, and instead looked at Mom with big eyes as if to say, *Oh my God, she really is that out of it.*

During one of my last days, I started to talk about Broadway and Elton John and how much I adored him. I remember Dr. Vadehra laughing and saying, "Look, she feels better!" I think I even laughed along a little. He is the only reason that I can associate any happy memories with that stay in the hospital.

Unfortunately, there were not many laughs there, because my condition was severe. There were also a lot of unknowns. But I only remember having one fleeting question—*Where is everyone?*

* * *

Because word had quickly spread about how serious my condition was, and how I was cognitively impaired, people didn't want to bother me. They were also afraid of me and what they would find, but I didn't know any of that.

I did have two good friends visit me. I don't remember anything other than they were there. Charlene came one of the first days and sat by Sean under the window, to the left of my bed. My friend Lena came later and sat on my right side. I can picture both of them in the room.

Charlene is a nurse, so she was probably better prepared for what I would look and sound like, but Lena was uncomfortable. A year later, Lena and I talked about it. She felt bad even telling me, but she didn't want to visit me. Her mother, Denise, my case manager, told her to do it for Sean. Lena said it was awkward being around me because I was so out of it. My family said that, based on how fast she was talking, you could tell she was uneasy. As she told me how painful it was, I choked back tears to tell her I'd never forget she was there and how much it meant to me.

It all started after I was released from the psychiatric ward. Sean became the gatekeeper, and all questions and concerns went through him. Ashley frequently checked in with Sean about how I was doing and what I was capable of understanding. Lacie witnessed my demise and lack of comprehension firsthand while taking care of me. Mike, Betsy, and the law firm knew the details, but offered only a pithy public position that I was out of the office indefinitely on medical leave. Sean, my family, and the few friends in our circle were all very protective of me and my reputation.

Their protection continued for many months after my release. Some people didn't know what they were going to get with me, and some didn't understand the gravity of my illness. Some people feared the worst or were afraid of me, so they stayed away. Some people demanded to see me and couldn't understand why I wasn't up for company. Sean vigilantly directed traffic to not overwhelm me or embarrass me, and people mostly honored that.

* * *

I was released from the hospital on Wednesday, March 30, in the early afternoon. I don't remember anything about my discharge or leaving.

I rode home with Sean and Mom in our van. When we got home, my friend Shelby met us at the house to give me a haircut. I only remember that Shelby cut an enormous amount of hair off as I sat at the far end of our kitchen table. She told me she would donate it to a charity that makes wigs for kids with cancer, and I was pleased about that.

Over a year later, Shelby and I talked about her experience. When she arrived, I was sitting on a lawn chair on the back deck, just staring. I asked her to cut my hair like the rock star P!nk. I was adamant that she do it that day. P!nk's hair is cool, but it's a commitment to a very short and striking style. Mom and Shelby looked at each other and said, *No way,* nonverbally, so they redirected me and convinced me that Shelby couldn't give me that style because she didn't have her clippers with her. Shelby didn't want to do such a thing to me when she could tell I wasn't in a good state of mind.

I had graduated high school with Shelby's brother, Seth, so I asked her about Seth and how he was doing. When she brought up Seth again, I didn't seem to understand who she was talking about. I was also very quiet. Shelby has known me for years, so she didn't miss the gravity of the situation. She saw a different person that day and called to report the same to her mother, a longtime family friend. And before she left, I reminded her to bring her clippers next time. I didn't get a rock star haircut, but it was much shorter and easier to manage.

Ashley came over to the house that afternoon to help Sean and to look for my health care directive. At that time, there was still fear of my incompetence or that I would die, so Ashley wanted our family to be prepared, especially for any trip to Mayo. I have no memory of her that day.

Thankfully, even though my time in the hospital was a little prickly between my family and Sean as it related to my going to Mayo, it all worked out fine and for the best. And it was a good thing that everyone was able to work together, because if any direction would have been needed from my health care directive, it was nowhere to be found.

After they had checked me into the psychiatric ward, Ashley had gone through my work desk for important documents and brought it all to our house to give to Sean. When the discussion came up about my health care directive, I was already in the hospital after my seizure, and no one had a copy.

Ashley and Sean began looking for it, to no avail. It was not in my home cabinet, amongst our wills and all other legal documents, and it wasn't at work in my file cabinet. Neither Mike nor Erica could find an electronic version on the server. Sean asked the hospital, assuming it was on file from when I had my children, but the hospital did not have a copy either. It had completely vanished.

Based upon the impeccable organization of everything in my office and at home, and because only my health care directive was missing, Ashley began to worry that I had purposefully destroyed it for some morbid reason. Sean wasn't too alarmed by the situation because he knew I had one, and he remembered my talking about it. Given that he was still in crisis mode for my life, it didn't faze him or alarm him the way it did Ashley. Its absence was very scary for Ashley, and she couldn't believe that we didn't have it through my two hospitalizations.

Had I been competent during their search, I could have led them to the health care directive, which was admittedly buried in an odd place after I took it with me to the hospital for the birth of my first child. I thought a copy was made then, but apparently it wasn't. As Sean and Ashley ripped the house apart looking for it, I was unaware of their mission, and they definitely didn't ask me for help. Months later, I found it with ease in a file box in the basement closet with my baby's hospitable discharge papers.

* * *

The five days I spent in the hospital were some of the most pivotal in my life, and I had no idea. I know I didn't grasp the enormity of the situation at all. I think I was just happy to get out of the boring hospital and go home to my kids. I don't remember being fearful of being back at home, but my family was scared that my life hung in the balance. We didn't yet have a concrete plan for treatment or know when I could go to the Mayo Clinic. They were overcome with *what's next* and *what if?*

CHAPTER 22

Upon my release, I still had a lot of physical and mental challenges. I was also on a lot of medication. I was discharged with seizure medication, pain medication, the anti-depression and anti-anxiety medication that I was started on in the psychiatric ward, and medication to sleep.

On May 31, Mom journaled: "Jackie slept all night. We walk around the block–I hold her arm – still unsteady. Had some visitors. Jackie still has trouble following a conversation. She listens a lot or looks at me to answer."

I slept fine at home upon my release, and I didn't have the insomnia or thrashing around like I did before. The only thing that gave me a challenge in bed was my shoulder pain and immobility. I remember once when I swore, my neighbor Kathy was standing over my bed trying to give me mail. But I woke up and realized I was dreaming, and that ended that. I didn't go back to any of the recurring dreams, hallucinations or paranoia that I had leading up to my seizure. My seizure seemed to reset me in a lot of ways, and more than just reducing my shaking. I slept and was less anxious and confused.

The visitors who came over the first few days all brought meals for our family. My brother Mike set up a "Meal-Train" online so people could sign up to bring us dinner. Up until the third meal when my high school friend Jill came over, and only sporadically after that, I don't remember people dropping off meals. Jill walked over to where I was sitting in my recliner, gave me a very gentle hug, and said, "You don't deserve this."

I remember seeing my friend and priest, Monsignor Gene Linde-mann. I asked Sean to call him to come over, as I hadn't seen a priest since Fr. Chris in the psychiatric ward. I had known him since I was a kid when he was at the church in a neighboring town. I don't remember much about his visit, but the look of genuine concern on his face was readily apparent, even to me. I was still unable to process what went on around me, but I could somewhat read the situations. I could feel that he was alarmed for me, but I couldn't help ease his mind. If anything, I made it worse. As we were all sitting around the table talking, I just got up and walked away to my recliner to sit and stare. My behavior and flat affect were very much unlike the usual Jackie that people were used to. Monsignor Gene was alarmed. He looked at Mom and said, "I'm really worried about her."

On June 1, Mom journaled: "I get Jackie showered, dressed, etc. The kids go on walks with us. Hard cuz they walk in front of her, and it throws her off. Distractions, fast movement is tough on her brain. Some guy walking with a big dog upsets her."

Beginning in the hospital and until about the end of August, either Sean or Mom had to get me in and out of the shower and help me wash up, dry off, and get dressed. Between my broken shoulder and how unsteady I was, it was impossible for me to do it all on my own. Initially upon my release, they put a folding chair in the shower stall because I was too weak to stand. Our shower was a step above the floor, so I needed a lot of help to get in and out to not trip and fall. We were all scared of my falling, so it took a lot of teamwork.

One day, Sean and I tried to sit down at the desk in my home office to pay some bills, which I always paid the first week of the month, and it was a disaster. I tried hard to help, but I felt bad because I knew I was nearly incompetent, and Sean grew frustrated. I had always taken care of all of our expenses and financial planning, and suddenly I couldn't do or remember anything. We couldn't even get on my laptop because it was password protected. I was finally able to get the password from my law firm planner, but when we attempted to login to websites to pay the bills, that was also problematic because it was hard for us to get into my password vault. Even with a cheat sheet I had previously made for

Sean in the event something happened to me, we still had difficulties and finally had to give it a rest. It was a small moment in time, but it was clear that I had been greatly relied upon by my family and could not perform for them, no matter how much I wanted to.

If Sean and I would have had to go on that way, with me being so unreliable and unsteady, our lives together would have been challenging. I've heard about couples losing their marriage after one person is diagnosed with autoimmune encephalitis. By the grace of God, and Sean's strength and compassion, Sean and I remain happily married.

It is my recollection that it was in the days after I got out of the hospital that I had a profound revelation. Mom and Sean don't remember it, but, in their defense, the conversation probably happened multiple times, yet I only remember the time it finally registered for me.

I can barely picture my sitting at my spot at the table and Mom and Sean moving about in the kitchen. I asked them a question about my mental illness and my stint in the psychiatric ward. I can hear their emphatic reply, "No, Jackie, you were never mentally ill. You didn't belong there. It was the autoimmune encephalitis."

My reaction was straight out of a cartoon. A bubble appeared over my head with a single lightbulb, and an invisible hand pulled the chain. Then the light blinked on, and I loudly responded, "O-o-o-o-o-o-o-h-h." It was the exact moment that I grasped my illness.

Overall, the days after I got out of the hospital were long for everyone. We hoped to talk to Dr. Dunnigan and continued to wait and wonder about my getting into the Mayo Clinic. On the evening of Sunday, June 3, to Sean's great relief, Dr. Dunnigan called him. He had received my hospital records and wanted an update. He told Sean that his office would be in contact with Sean to set up an appointment.

On June 3, Mom journaled: "Jackie comes down at 6:30 am. Dr. Dunnigan called to see how Jackie's doing. I was gonna go home, but she needs me."

On June 4, she wrote: "Waited all day to hear from Dr. Dunnigan. He called at 4:30 p.m. Going to start IV steroids tomorrow! Hopefully we are going forward–Jackie is sick and frustrated."

CHAPTER 23

On the morning of June 5, Sean and Mom accompanied me to the clinic to see Dr. Dunnigan, where they spent the duration of the appointment discussing my working diagnosis of autoimmune encephalitis, my prognosis, and whether to begin treatment. Sean and Mom desperately wanted me to start getting steroids for treatment, and Dr. Dunnigan agreed that, at that point, they had to act. The problem was that Dr. Dunnigan still didn't have the results from the encephalitis panel, nor did he have the results of my cerebral spinal fluid that had all been sent to Mayo's lab for analysis. My family feared that if I started on steroids and anything happened to the labs taken a few weeks prior, that we would never have a clear picture of my diagnosis because the steroids would alter my body.

What helped make the decision was that Dr. Dunnigan was able to speak with one of the neurologists at Mayo whom he knew, and that doctor agreed that starting me on methylprednisolone (IV steroids) was justified. Dr. Dunnigan then outlined a plan to give me four 1,000 mg IV treatments daily that week and thoroughly discussed the known risks associated with such high doses of steroids.

Mom and Sean felt like beginning with steroids was more than justified. They believed it was an absolute necessity and that we were at a critical juncture for me. So even without the lab results and fear of my body altering, and with the associated risks of steroids, they emphatically asked Dr. Dunnigan to order the treatment.

He also ordered a CT scan of my chest, abdomen, and pelvis to check for a tumor. He told my family that the scan was important to make sure there were no tumors lurking in me, cancerous or otherwise, that had possibly ignited my immune system to start fighting against my brain.

I only remember a few things from that appointment. I felt like Dr. Dunnigan droned on about the possible side effects from steroids, but all I really picked up on was possible issues with my joints. And at the end, he told me I should eat a banana every day. I didn't really understand why, but I heard him say it, and because I'm a rule follower, I ate a banana nearly every day for a really long time.

At the conclusion of the appointment, I looked at him and very sincerely asked him whether he believed I would have another seizure. Even though I still lived in a fog, the words *grand mal seizure* kept me on edge. I was petrified of having another seizure and feared what it would do to me. In a way that I've now come to know as the typical, dry but funny fashion of him, he stared at me intensely and sternly said, "Don't!"

I took that to heart and decided I better not have another seizure.

* * *

After my appointment, we slowly walked into the infusion center's waiting room located inside the clinic. I remember the sights and sounds of oncology everywhere, including the sick patients. I recall frail looking women with coverings on their heads and elderly couples. The treatment center had the same antiseptic feel that I was growing accustomed to: a cold, concrete hospital floor, yellowish or brownish walls, and blinds over thick windows. But it felt even more sterile and even more serious. What attempted to look comfortable were the over-stuffed brown leather chairs, but the beeping machines and IV poles placed next to the seats stole the attention.

I took my spot in a chair not too far from the door, and the nurse promptly brought me some warm, hospital grade, white blankets. She then started an IV in my left arm, the only good arm I had, to be subjected to the next month's abuse of IVs and blood draws. Once the IV was inserted, I was slowly blasted with 1,000 mg of steroids over the course of an hour. Sean and Mom took turns waiting with me during the treatment, while I ate suckers to keep a gross taste out of my mouth.

Sean took a picture of me, and while I look a little uncomfortable in my recliner with my sling and IV in, by all accounts I look like myself, just with shorter hair. Sean posted the photo of me in my college alma mater shirt on Facebook with the caption "Day 1 of treatment!"

During the treatment, I had to go to the bathroom and asked Mom to accompany me. Also accompanying me was the reality of how helpless I was. So was the enormity of where I was, and how sick I was, because I could see cancer patients receiving infusions all around me. I gingerly walked to the bathroom, rolling my IV with, and Mom followed me in so she could wipe my butt. It distinctly registered in my mind that my life wasn't glamorous.

Your brain has a barrier specifically set up to keep things away from it, but with that high dose of steroids, the brain barrier can be penetrated, and that was the goal for me. I'm not sure if we expected to see such immediate results, but we did. I don't remember feeling the immense improvement like I felt on day two, but it was instantly noticeable to my family. Mom journaled: "Sean and I took Jackie to her first infusion–1,000 mg solu-medrol. Afterwards she started talking more & more energy."

* * *

June 6, day two of the treatments, is the day that really stands out to me as the one where I felt my mind rally and start to go back to normal. It was a great feeling! That day, Sean posted a picture of me where I look much more comfortable in my shoulder brace and in my chair. I'm wearing a Stebbins Mulloy Law Firm T-shirt and listening to music on my phone, while eating a sucker and giving the peace sign. Sean's comment was "Day 2 of treatment: Suckers and Elton John music…the first sign of normalcy from Jackie."

After my second treatment, the light turned back on for me. The fog lifted, and it felt like my brain was once again my own. I didn't think much of it at the time, but I did something unbelievable that day, right after I left my brown chair. I went downtown to the polling location and participated in the state's primary election. Since I had turned eighteen, I've never missed voting in a state, local, or national election, including the time I didn't even have a car and rode my bike a few miles on a low tire. My friend Nancy was running for reelection for her city commissioner position, and I had hosted a fundraiser for her in April. I wanted to make sure that she had my vote. I walked very slowly into City Hall with Sean and Mom, and I cast my ballot. Exactly seven days prior, I had been released from the hospital and still suffered from cognitive impairment. The gravity of the situation went over my head but did not go unnoticed by my family. They were all ecstatic! Mom journaled: "Jackie and Sean voted early. Jackie is much better. It's like we have her back after 2 treatments! We take walks in the warm weather."

At home later that afternoon, I remember Kathy commented at least a few times that I was back to myself. It was very good news for me to hear! I also remember going through some billing issues on the phone with the hospital at the kitchen table with Mom next to me. I got a little angry when the woman was not understanding the issue, and Mom told me to calm down. She wondered if the steroids were already affecting my mood. I believed it was probably pent-up anger after being incompetent for the prior month, so I didn't think a thing about it.

Unfortunately, that day was not all roses. With the awakening in my mind, reality started to crash down on me, and it felt like more than a ten-thousand-pound gorilla. I started to process all that had gone on without my knowing and that I was completely out of the loop.

People knew that I was sick because my story was growing publicly and being shared via social media and word of mouth. Sean started a CaringBridge page for me on May 28. He couldn't keep up with calls and messages, so he decided to publish my story to a wider audience. We began to receive an enormous amount of cards and financial donations, on top of the meals people were bringing us, and my sister-in-law, Kelly, started a Go Fund Me page for our family on May 27. I was very thankful, but immediately became overwhelmed by how public my condition was and how many misconceptions were possibly floating around.

I was also gaining notoriety in the local medical community. Dr. Dunnigan told me, "You were the case study of the week and the talk of both hospitals." I had never aspired to that type of recognition.

What sent me over the top that day, and I remember it well, was Ashley coming over to our house to talk with Sean. I chatted with her and then she took Sean into my office, and they shut the door to talk. That was all it took, and I erupted into tears and panic. I had not been at work since May 8, and I had no idea about what was going on at the firm. I hadn't talked to Mike since I went into the psychiatric ward, so I was worried that he was angry at me and unsettled with all the chaos that I felt I had caused. I realized that if I wasn't working, I couldn't make money, and I had solely supported our family. I knew I had built-up deferred earnings, but they were not infinite. I also knew I had long-term disability insurance, but not working scared me, mostly because my job exclusively provided my family with health insurance and stability.

I thought back to all the nights I had lain awake with my insomnia and worried that I would lose my law firm, my livelihood, my career, and my home, and I panicked more. It was all going to come true. I was going to lose everything.

When Ashley left, I freaked out. I told Sean and Kathy over and over that everything I had worked for was lost. I wailed with tears. I was fraught and began shaking. I demanded to know what Ashley was talking to Sean about behind closed doors because I finally realized that no one had told me anything for a month, and I was unsure of nearly all aspects of my life.

Sean calmed me down and told me they were just talking about everything they had been discussing for the past few weeks: our bills, my role in the law firm, health insurance, and the disability claim that I would have to make. He reassured me that no one was mad and that Ashley was still trying to help him get everything situated. Sean could tell that I was very upset and was cognizant of my surroundings. He called Ashley later to tell her that I was with it again and that, going forward, I needed to be included in discussions. Ashley was happy to hear that I was back and could start engaging in the conversations. But they both worried about overwhelming me.

People had been discussing me and making decisions about me behind my back, and right in front of me, and I had no idea. Once that sunk in, it hurt. I knew that Sean was my gatekeeper, and my agency had diminished.

That day started the doom that I felt ad nauseam, day and night, for over a year, and it was something that I couldn't shake. My persistent thoughts were: I let the firm down, I let my family down, I left everyone at the law firm and they're angry at me, everything I've worked for is lost, and my livelihood is gone. The guilt and fear immediately overtook me and went on for longer than I care to admit. I could barely even focus on the situation staring me in the face, which was my own health. All I could think of was *Oh my God, what have I done to everyone around me?* It's hard to explain how hard the reality of my situation hit me that day, but it did. It felt like a missile had hit me, and I exploded.

CHAPTER 24

On June 7, day three of the treatments, my bad luck had returned. I underwent the CT scan after my infusion to check for tumors. The good news was that I didn't have any tumors present. But there was also bad news. The scan revealed two blood clots in my right lung.

Dr. Dunnigan called my primary physician, Dr. Froelich, to inform her of the situation, and we all hoped that she could see me immediately. I was placed in a wheelchair at the clinic and quickly taken for a leg ultrasound to check for any clots in my legs. I was then whisked away to see Dr. Froelich.

I hadn't seen her since my last appointment in April, but she had been briefed on my condition. When she got into the room, she gave me a big hug and seemed in disbelief over my condition. I'll never forget some of the first words out of her mouth—"That damn colitis." I agreed. I had a strong fear that my colitis had set off a chain reaction, and it ended up imploding my brain.

She told us that the leg ultrasound images weren't very clear, but it looked as if I also had a clot or two in my right femoral vein. Considering the gravity of the situation with clots in my chest and leg, she acted quickly and prescribed a blood thinning medication. She also asked that I take it easy and told me that I would have to stop walking and use a wheelchair when I was out. I was immediately crushed. I had just seen a faint glimmer of hope for normalcy during the past two days. Strolling through the neighborhood with Mom and the kids was one of the few things I could do to pass the time, and it was now prohibited.

When we got home, I sat on the couch and pondered it all. I was mostly angry that I couldn't even walk anymore. I don't remember having any *why me?* moments until that precise time after the news of the blood clots. Then they rushed me.

Sean updated the CaringBridge page, and, based upon the feedback, it felt like the whole world was again scared of what felt like my impending death. It was the first time I felt others' fear and devastation. Over and over, people refrained that I just couldn't catch a break. The reality of the fragility of my health, and the magnitude of all that was out of my control, hit me like a bag of bricks. My friend Jack's comment felt particularly poignant: "We continue to hold our collective breath." I knew people were scared that I could just die, and now I was too.

I started to question my own mortality, and it weighed heavily on me. I had already escaped most of the worst, but my fears grew because my mind was coming back. It was the difference between not having the ability to comprehend that I was knocking on death's door versus understanding that I was going through a near-death experience. And on top of it, without my tests back and without a planned trip to the Mayo Clinic, I didn't feel that my diagnosis of autoimmune encephalitis was even concrete. There was still the nagging feeling that pulled at me and my family of *What if it's something else?* We were all just waiting for the other shoe to drop.

Mom journaled: "Jackie had a bad day. Couldn't get her IV in. Had CT scan to check for tumors and they found blood clots in her right lung and one in her femoral vein."

* * *

I had my final IV treatment that Friday, June 8. I didn't like being in the infusion room, because it scared and depressed me. Because of the scarves on women's heads and how loudly a skinny young man next to me snored through his treatment in work clothes, I felt despair and impending death all around me. I didn't want to be there, and I was sick of people digging in my left arm to start IVs from my non-cooperative veins.

The news didn't get much better that day when Dr. Froelich called to review my radiology reports with us. They confirmed the clots in my chest and leg. The CT scan also revealed three fractured vertebrae in my back. We were astonished at the breaks, but we also laughed because it explained why I kept asking people to itch my back when I got out of the hospital. Overall, the news continued to feel unreal.

The one bright spot that day was in one of the first personal emails I received since getting sick, and it was the first one I was able to read by myself. It was hard for me to see on my phone or to type, so I didn't do it often, but I checked my email that day and had a powerful message from Mark Schneider.

Mark was a phenomenal trial lawyer in North Dakota and was the chairman of the Democratic Party when I became the vice-chairwoman. I was instantly taken to Mark in our work together, and I deeply admired him. He wrote:

> Dear Jackie: So sorry to hear of your health issues. Hope Mayo works its magic for you. Know that you are in the thoughts and best wishes of all the Schneiders. Get well, Jackie. There are many folks who need your commitment to the law, your party, and a better society. Mark

Mark's words touched me deeply and inspired me the moment I read them. I recognized that I had countless friends like Mark, who wanted me to return to the force I had become, and I had to deliver. A glimmer of hope came over me that everything would someday return to normal. It was just a long way away. But there was also a nagging feeling that sat at the bottom of my soul that told me I wouldn't ever be able to return to practice. I tried not to let it weigh on me, and, instead, I cherished Mark's words. I will never delete that email.

That weekend was one of the longest I had ever endured. I was confined to the couch. And it was the weekend, so no doctors could call me, which meant I wouldn't get any news about anything, most notably from the Mayo Clinic. To occupy our time, Mom and I began filling out my application for my long-term disability insurance, which was quite a chore. My health was especially burdening my mind, but my fear of complete financial ruin was in a very close second. Now I had disability insurance to worry about too. My family would only be able to survive if the insurance money came through. I felt like I was going to explode.

By Sunday evening, I developed a massive headache. I could barely sit, stand, or lie down. So I panicked because I knew that the night I had my seizure was after I had my terrible headache from the spinal tap. We called Dr. Froelich, and she believed I was crashing from having the IV steroids for four days and then nothing. She wondered whether I needed to start on daily oral steroids for more consistency. Thankfully, I had an IV treatment and appointment with Dr. Dunnigan the next day, but I spent the night in a frenzy that I was going to have another seizure.

* * *

On Monday, June 11, we went to see Dr. Dunnigan for the first visit after my week of treatments. He was pleased that I believed my cognition had improved, and my family agreed that the steroids had turned me back around. He noted me as more spontaneous and smiling more. He found it interesting that my tremors were mostly alleviated after the seizure and that my family believed it had reset me.

I didn't have a seizure the night before as I fretted about, but I told him about crashing over the weekend. He then prescribed 60 mg of daily oral prednisone, beginning after I took my final IV treatment that day.

He also ordered blood work to look at the strength of my seizure medication. The results showed that I didn't have enough, so he increased my dosage. I wasn't thrilled about the higher dose and daily steroids, but I knew it was all part of the process, and I had little say in it. I had to get over my aversion to medication in order to save my life. There was no room for questions or arguments.

Sean took a photograph of me that day in my infusion chair wearing a "Heidi Heitkamp for United States Senate" shirt. It was the peppiest I looked in all the photos. Sean posted the picture with the comment "Feeling tough in the Heidi shirt today." A few of Heidi's staffers were tagged in the post, which resulted in a big surprise for me later that day.

When I got home that afternoon, I did what I had grown accustomed to doing, which was sitting outside in the sun in my lawn chair. When I got situated, I listened to a voicemail I had from North Dakota's Senator Heidi Heitkamp. She had seen my picture and joked about where I got such a cool shirt. She laughed her big, warm Heidi laugh and then seriously gave me a "What the hell, girl? Take care of yourself. And if there's anything I can do, let me know." She even told me that she loved me to death. I saved the voicemail and smiled all day. She had taken the time to call me when she had important business in the senate and was running for reelection. That voicemail definitely lifted my rather bleak spirits and again reminded me that I had a lot of wonderful friends who were going to help pull me through my crisis.

Mom left for home that day after living with us for nearly a month. She journaled: "Went to Jackie's appointment with Dr. Dunnigan and then Jack and I went home. It's been 1 day short of 4 weeks. Jackie is sad and angry. Me too."

I was distraught when she left, but I knew she needed to get back to her own life, and I couldn't keep her at our house forever. Sean and I were both nervous about taking care of me by ourselves. Fortunately for us, Kathy stayed a while longer, so we at least had one extra set of hands to help with the kids and around the house. And I told myself that I would have to be a little more independent without Mom there to meet my every need.

* * *

Overall, the week felt long, boring, scary, and a few more frustrations set in. After my release from the hospital, I became terrified that I was losing my vision. It was hard for my eyes to focus, and things were very blurry, especially print in books. It also wasn't easy for me to see my computer screen, but my phone screen was especially challenging. If I tried to read a book or look at a screen, I only grew frustrated. We quickly made an appointment to see my eye doctor.

I saw him on June 13, and he had all good news. I had just had my vision checked in October 2017, and my sight remained the same. I was relieved, and I hoped my eyes would start coming around quickly so I could try to ease back into reading. I didn't dive right back into reading books though, because it was also hard on my brain. Which meant that my list of things to do continued to be very short.

I also saw Dr. Pierce that week. He told me that my break was still healing and wouldn't be fully healed for about ten more weeks. I had to continue in my brace but could start light physical therapy. I was not excited about physical therapy because it had been hard and painful work after I had surgery years ago. And this time, I had to rehab a dislocation on top of a break when I was unsteady, highly medicated, and had a brain illness.

The highlight of any appointments came in the form of my meeting Stephanie Macdonald again. By that point, I understood that she had saved my life. She came to get us in the waiting room, and when I saw her I said, "Oh yeah, I remember you now." When we got back to her office, I told her, "Thank you for saving my life" and gave her a big hug.

Because of the high doses of prednisone, insomnia set in that week. It felt different, so it didn't scare me like it had while I was getting sick, but it was still miserable. My days began at anywhere from 1:00 a.m. to 2:00 a.m. and sometimes started as early as 12:00 a.m. I couldn't do much in the middle of the night, except watch television, so I asked Sean for a tutorial on how to run our Smart TV and how to use Netflix. I never had much time for television and didn't watch a lot of movies, so it was all new to me.

For the first few days, it only felt like an inconvenience. But as time went on, it became my heavy burden. The all-nighters were my continuous reality until December 2018.

It was not only hard to sleep at night, it was also hard to rest much during the day. After I saw Dr. Pierce, I slept for about thirty minutes in the afternoon, and I couldn't believe how much it helped. It was the first time I had napped since before January 2018, and I needed it. After that, I diligently tried to rest every afternoon.

And so started my daily routine of being fatigued day and night but unable to sleep much. I could not work, I could not drive, I could not walk, I couldn't use my right arm, and I could hardly see to read for more than a few minutes. I was unsteady and felt miserable and drunk. I couldn't see my phone or the computer to play on the internet, and I was up most of the night. I worried about my health, my mortality, what would happen to my children and husband if I died, the law firm, and our finances. It was a dreadful existence.

The only good news came later that week when Mom, who was frustrated by not hearing from Mayo, called them. She found out that I had been accepted and was able to make a neurology appointment for June 18. We all leapt for joy, yet at the same time we were frightened. I was finally going to get a conclusive diagnosis and learn more about my own fate. The weight of my world felt staggering, but I took some action.

I picked up the first journal I began writing in before and neatly wrote down my symptoms to prepare for the upcoming clinic visits:

fatigue

tongue tingles when I drink

bite my mouth @ dinner

worn out by 5pm

shakey

anxiety & nervous

loud overwhelms me—over stimulated—reactions slow

kids make me sensitive & irritable (god I'm sorry)

don't like things by my face

some blury eye sight—can be hard to read

seems like good days & bad days

can get moody & agitated

no shoulder mobility

(immunity & nerves)

don't leave house

struggle names of Doc's

still some memory loss

search for words

awake all hours

headaches from roids & lack of sleep

loss of focus &

multitask

forget what I set out to do

CHAPTER 25

The day before we left for Mayo was Father's Day. I tried to make it an enjoyable day for Sean, and the kids helped me make him a cake. Kathy and Shelly arrived that day to stay at our home and watch the kids in our absence. We assumed our trip would take at least the entire week, if not more. We all tried hard to keep everything at home as normal as possible so the kids wouldn't be affected by my health, but kids are perceptive, and ours were no exception. They knew something was still wrong with me, so it was tough to tell them that we had to go away for a week. On top of that, our nerves were palpable to everyone, especially them, and I didn't want to leave them for so long.

The *what-ifs* raced through my mind, and my emotions poured out. I sat on the front porch by myself that night. I remember big, hot tears running down my face and my heart racing. I was so overwhelmed that I didn't know what to do with myself. I tried to listen to music for the first time in months. I went back to the songs I had downloaded in March, especially "Let it Be" and "The Boxer." The music comforted me and fueled my fears of sickness and death all at the same time. For some reason, that odd combination was helpful.

I had my journal out, and the inspiration was there, so I began jotting down some thoughts again. The first entry is very legibly printed:

> Night before Mayo:
>
> been shaky for 2 days
>
> been irritable and anxious

tonight it all set in—I'm scared

listened to some tunes

#letitbe

hope to not reinvent the wheel on tests!

hope to have a dx and tx—what's the plan

what is the status of my life?!

just hold hope and faith

While sitting on the porch, I also made two important phone calls. The first was to try to catch my friend Mac Schneider, Mark's son, who is an attorney and was running for US Congress. Upon his hearing the news of my illness, he immediately called Sean and offered up his pro bono legal services to me. It was a very generous offer, and I believed I was going to need counsel to help me navigate my complicated life. I left him a voicemail, and then I made one of the hardest phone calls of my life. I called Mike to talk to him for the first time since I had left for the psychiatric ward.

Because we hadn't spoken in a while, and after what had transpired for both of us, I felt very afraid to talk to him. I started sobbing immediately and felt like I was startling him. I finally said it—"I don't think I can come back, Mike. I don't even know if I'm disabled yet." Between my tears and his long pauses, the conversation was painful. I felt like my heart was breaking. He calmed me down, wished me the best at Mayo, and we said we'd be in touch.

* * *

The next morning, after saying tough goodbyes to the kids, Mom, Sean, and I took off early for Rochester. From our house to the clinic, it's almost exactly a nine-hour drive. With the way my head felt, and my immobilized right arm that was hard to prop up, or leave down, the trip was very long. The nights there were also long, as I had to try to not wake Mom and Sean in our hotel suite while I was up all night. I mostly clung to the power of prayer that week.

Because I was raised Catholic, I had prayed the rosary many times with someone leading me. But until I got sick, I had never prayed it on my own. Before we left, I dug through my jewelry box to find my grandmother's rosary and another to take with me. I decided it was time to learn how to pray the rosary by myself. I was scared for my life and felt like there was so much that was out of my hands, and that didn't make sense, so I turned to prayer.

Even though the rosary is mostly comprised of the same three prayers over and over, I still had to use a book to do it by myself. But it helped me pass the time during my long nights, and, because I was still fidgety with my hands, I liked the way it felt to roll the coarse beads around on my fingertips. I'm glad it was something that I turned to so quickly, as it became a very powerful tool in my recovery.

* * *

On Tuesday, June 19, we ventured across the street from our hotel to the main clinic in downtown Rochester. It looms above the otherwise modest buildings in a city of only one hundred thousand people. What you note from the outside are the beautiful, bluish windows.

In my opinion, Mayo was the place you landed when you had a condition that made everyone throw up their hands, or a diagnosis so rare and severe that you were immediately sent there because no one else wanted to touch you. And I believed it to be one of the finest medical centers on earth.

As we headed toward my neurology appointment, I was humbled to be there, but I was overwhelmed. The people around me seemed very sick, and I was confined to a wheelchair. I belonged at the Mayo Clinic because of a rare brain condition, and that sense of belonging frightened me.

My first appointment, and probably the most important one that I had during my four days at the clinic, was with Dr. Anastasia Zekeridou, a neurologist. I was instantly fond of her because she was bright, knowledgeable, and easy to talk to. I knew she was going to take good care of me. She also told me I could call her "Dr. Z" for short, and because I was still struggling with names, I took her up on that. After introductions, she let me know she had reviewed my records and that all my labs were back. All three of us instantly sat up in our chairs and waited to hear the news.

She said I didn't have any of the dreaded autoimmune encephalitis antibodies present. At that moment, my mind went wild, and I wondered what fresh sort of medical hell I was facing if it wasn't the devil that we had barely come to know. I bellowed out a response, "What? Does this mean I don't have autoimmune encephalitis?" She calmed me down and told me to be patient, as we had a long way to go.

We began by going through my medical history. Sean was so used to interjecting and answering for me that I had to pat his knee a few times to remind him that I was fine to answer. After she obtained the information, she asked me to undergo some testing. The dreaded neurological examinations were back.

Overall, I did just fine. I could do math in my head and remember things or lists that she told me. I could feel when she was manipulating my toes, what she placed in my hands, and when she drew imaginary symbols on my skin. I knew I was under scrutiny but was able to make it through without crying, and I drew a clock with ease. I scored a 35/38. I lost one point for incorrect math and two points for my recollection. While my physical neurological examination was a bit limited because of my right shoulder, I did great.

She then left for a consultation with Dr. Andrew McKeon, also a neurologist. One of the Mayo Clinic's greatest gifts is its emphasis on the collaborative process. The Mayo collaboration process was worth its weight in gold when Dr. Z returned with Dr. McKeon to finalize our visit and discuss my next steps.

I had an immediate appreciation for Dr. McKeon. He is from Ireland and has a remarkably cool Irish accent. He is very approachable, but he's so brilliant he makes me a little nervous. He asked me a few follow-up questions and then told us that it was their opinion that I had made a convincing case for autoimmune encephalitis, even without the antibodies present. With the rapid progression of my behavioral problems, insomnia, cognitive problems, and seizures, I fit the mold. Thus, my diagnosis of seronegative autoimmune encephalitis. And because I'm seronegative (no detectable antibodies), I'm actually a rarity within a rare disease.

Dr. McKeon was pleased that I responded so well to early steroid treatment and had made such rapid progress. It was his belief that I would make a full recovery but that the recovery would take a long time, probably up to a year or more and that it would take me the longest time to get that last 10 percent or so toward my 100 percent. The news was some of the best I had ever heard. Sean, Mom, and I all felt elated at the mention of full recovery!

Dr. McKeon also delivered good news to us in that he didn't believe that the autoimmune encephalitis would return. Although he could make no guarantees that it would never return, he seemed confident that upon my successful treatment with steroids over the course of the next year and a half that I would stay in remission. Hopefully, I was one and done. I was ecstatic that he seemed genuinely confident that the nightmare wouldn't return, but it was also hard for me to hear that he couldn't say "never again."

They ordered me to continue with the 60 mg of daily prednisone and my anti-seizure medication. After three months, I would be allowed to begin tapering my prednisone by 10 mg each month. Once I was down to just 10 mg, I would then taper by 1 mg each month. Quick math proved that I would be on steroids for a long time, but it didn't seem to concern me that day because I had no real experience with prolonged steroid use and all the brutal side effects, especially for a woman. I was also a long way from getting off my anti-seizure medication.

Both physicians were very happy with Dr. Dunnigan's thorough workup and evaluation of me and extended their confidence in my continued treatment with him. We were already very confident in him, but it was also quite reassuring to have my Mayo Clinic physicians verify that he was doing a remarkable job.

We had a lot to do that week to paint a picture of good health for me. I was sent away with a long list of appointments for cancer screening, including a pelvic and breast screen, an endoscopy to look at my stomach, and a complete PET scan. Both physicians wanted to rule out the possibility that cancer was lurking its ugly head somewhere in my body and that it was the reason for my tripped immune system. I was also asked to see the cardiovascular department about my blood clots and the sleep department for my insomnia. The to-do list was overwhelming, and all the appointments were not set in stone, so we had our work cut out for us.

Overall, we were all relieved with what seemed to be very good news on that first day, but we still had a lot of questions for my doctors about my rare and complicated illness. I walked out of the appointment grumbling about how I knew I didn't have cancer. I repeatedly stated that I had autoimmune encephalitis and "that's it." Sean and Mom were so overjoyed by the words "autoimmune encephalitis diagnosis" and "full recovery" that they ignored my commentary.

* * *

The second morning, Wednesday, I had to do a blood draw. We got there at 6:00 a.m. and were some of the first in the line. I sat in my wheelchair and looked at a newspaper as Sean waited behind me. After waiting in line for about thirty minutes, the lab opened. When I saw an employee gesture for the next person to check in, I got up out of my wheelchair and raced to her desk. I could feel Sean's horror and others' stares around me, so I stopped and looked back and realized that a lady was in front of me, and I had just cut her off. And I had jumped out of a wheelchair to do so. I sheepishly walked back to her and apologized and allowed her to go ahead of me. I waited in line another minute or so and then graciously walked to the counter to check in for my blood draw.

My next appointment was with a physician's assistant about my blood clots, and it went very well. I was on the right path with my medication and would need to be on it at least as long as I treated for my autoimmune encephalitis. The best news of the day came when I asked him if I could resume activity and dump my wheelchair, and he said yes. That immediately changed my attitude, and I happily walked out of that appointment. Mom and Sean were also relieved because all I did was snip at them when they pushed me in the wheelchair.

That afternoon, we went to a local mall and walked around a little. I only made it into one store before I felt too weak and too uncomfortable to be out in public. It was short lived, so we went back to our room to relax there. I was only comfortable when I could sit on a bed or in a chair and read my book, write in my journal, listen to music, or pray the rosary. Being out in public for any prolonged amount of time was upsetting and hard for me.

I was still a little confused too. When I walked in and out of clinic rooms and our hotel room, I wasn't sure which room was mine or which way to go. I also struggled with the water knobs in the hotel. Our hotel was older, so the shower and the sink each had two knobs for hot and cold water, and you had to adjust them both to get a comfortable mix for warm water. The two sets were opposite of one another for the direction you had to turn them on and off, and I kept forgetting which way to turn. On Thursday morning, I attempted to shower by myself since I was up so early and nearly scalded myself when I couldn't figure out the knobs.

Thursday was a long day. I had an early blood draw, pelvic ultrasound, my first ever mammogram, and a PET scan late in the day. I was afraid of the mammogram, because I feared someone would harm my shoulder if they couldn't see my sling, so I asked Mom to accompany me. It felt like a disaster because it was hard for the technicians to position me around my injury, and it was challenging for me to hold the position. And we had hardly finished when we were escorted to a small room and told to wait. We assumed that we were going to hear bad news.

A radiologist came in later and sat down with us. She told us she saw calcification spots on my right breast and that she wanted to do a biopsy. She considered it an intermediate risk for cancer. I didn't like the word "intermediate." I was comforted, however, when I found out that sometimes calcification deposits resulted from impact to the breast or breast feeding. Between my days in high impact sports and the lengthy time I breastfed both of my children, I had encountered each, so I hoped for the best.

There was no way I could lie face down in the prone position with my right arm up, so doing the biopsy at that time wasn't possible. She stressed to us the importance of my getting a biopsy as soon as I was physically able to do so, and I agreed that I would.

Waiting for my PET scan that evening felt like an eternity. I was hungry, in pain, exhausted, and had a slight fear that I had cancer brewing in my body. The PET scan was also a fairly long process, which didn't help. The worst was the injection of the radioactive substance, which was weird to think about in and of itself. Not to mention the fact that I was told that for twenty-four hours after the test I would always need to flush the toilet twice after I used it. The actual scan didn't take as long as I feared it would, but it wasn't easy because I had to lie still, and my right arm shook because it was in an awkward position. I was relieved when it was all over.

* * *

The next morning, Friday, was my final appointment with Dr. Z to review the results from all the cancer screening I underwent. All I could think about was getting home to see my kids. I wanted out of Mayo, and I wanted to be at home where I could lie on the couch and watch TV while I was up at all hours of the night. The appointment was quick and held all good news. My PET scan came back negative, and so did all the other screens! We again went through the treatment plan for my steroids, and she reiterated that my recovery would take time and that, unfortunately, there was no real timetable for progress.

What stuck with me the most from the visit that day was one of the first things Dr. Z told me. I don't remember what prompted her, but she said what I needed to hear. As she gently placed her hand on my knee, she emphatically stated that I did not bring on autoimmune encephalitis. She said, "You did nothing wrong. You didn't make yourself sick."

The painful emotions from the past two months came flooding back to me in an instant. All the guilt and self-blame I had, especially in the psychiatric ward, that I had let my life get out of control or that I worked until I made myself sick, burst out of me, and I wept hard. She was very empathetic and listened to me when I said that, for a long time, I blamed myself for the downward spiral of my health and that those thoughts had seriously damaged me. I was just about as happy to hear that it wasn't my fault as I was to hear that I would make a full recovery.

We were all happy with the results and my orders for treatment and recovery, but we were happiest to get in the car and head for home. When we pulled into the garage later that night, the kids, up way past their bedtime, were waiting for us by the door. We were delighted to see them.

As I crawled into bed late and got up to watch TV on the couch early the next morning, I felt a sense of calm come over me that I was on the right path and that I could rise to the challenge ahead of me. I could make a full recovery.

Unfortunately, I didn't stay calm for long. The recovery process was more than anyone could have prepared me for.

PART III – THE ROAD TO RECOVERY

My rosary has broken and my beads have all slipped through.

"Sixty Years On" by Elton John

CHAPTER 26

The enormity of the situation and the severity of my illness took a while to completely set in and become reality for me. When it all came to a head, the future seemed bleak.

My world had crashed down around me, and I hardly knew myself. I began to ponder deep existential questions, such as *Will I get better? What exactly is better? Am I a different person?—Where is my life headed?*

On June 27, Sean accompanied me to Ken's accounting firm for a previously scheduled personal meeting. Yet this one was remarkably different from all others. Sean had never met Ken, so of course we had never met him together after our life had been firebombed. Our nerves were palpable, and I was very fragile.

We sat in the black, high-back chairs in the corner of the long table where I always sat to meet with Ken, but I wasn't wearing my usual blazer or suit. I was in red Nike gym shorts and a white tee. My short hair was behind a headband, and my immobilized right arm was black and blue and swollen all down to my hand.

He came in and warmly greeted both of us, but he seemed a little different to me that day. It wasn't all numbers as usual. We had more to cover. We chatted for a while about my health and recent events, but as we segued to the questions about our finances and life at the law firm, I had a massive breakdown. Sean did what he had grown accustomed to and gently placed his hand on my leg while I sobbed. I believed that I was humiliating myself in front of Ken, but I didn't care. I heaved out,

"This is all my fault. It's a mess. People have lost their jobs. And it's all because of me."

While Ken recognized my delicate state, he didn't let me off the hook. He wasn't going to hear a word from me about failure, nor allow me to give up. He said, "You gave people jobs," and he reminded me that my success in three years was more than he'd seen from about anyone.

He ended by saying, "The Jackie I know is not going to take this lying down. The Jackie I know is going to find a way back to the top."

I instantly hated him for those words. How dare he tell me that I could rise again, as I sat bawling in his fancy conference room. I was finished, and he needed to recognize that.

How dare he believe in me the way he had for years. How dare he push me back toward any success. Coming from such a well-respected person whom I greatly admired, how dare he continue to believe in me.

As we walked out of the glass doors, my numbed mind said, *Rise back to the top... huh. We'll see.*

* * *

My short-term worries were small brush fires, and my mind constantly dumped the gasoline. I spent most of my waking thoughts obsessing about my status as a practicing lawyer, my place in the law firm, and our money. In small whizzing visions, I saw my life in college and law school, and I saw the past nine years of practice. The pictures were of me working myself into frenzies to succeed.

The final image was always a detailed explosion. The joy of my triumphs met the disruption of my disease, and I saw the millions of colorful fragments erasing as they fell to the ground.

I no longer felt my drive. I felt defeated.

Deep down, I knew that I had already lost my career. Going back to my firm to be the person and lawyer that I was before seemed like a hopeless notion. I had no magic insight into my future, but I didn't believe that my health could ever again endure the stress of practice, clients, and management.

It was hard, because I knew what I did affected Mike too. My illness meant a big change in the master plan, and the larger hopes for our partnership and future were destroyed.

After some emotional conversations, Mike and I agreed that I would exit the firm. I tried to be at peace with the fact that I had to leave practice, give up my business and livelihood, and forego my goals because it was what I needed to do for my body and mind. But it hurt in an indescribable way.

I had nothing in my reserves to deplete, but the loss of my dreams found a way to endlessly pull from me.

My long-term worries took a back seat but silently gnawed at me. I wondered if I would ever reenter the workforce. I worried that my disease had scarred my children and that the effects would show over time. I questioned if I would recover as much as my doctors at Mayo told me I could. I pondered what it would look like to start anew, in my mid-thirties. I feared I wouldn't live to see my grandchildren.

A narrative found its way into my playback loop and repeatedly nagged *What if this is as good as it gets?*

All the stressors were more than I could bear. My head was clearer, and my mind began to slowly work again, but I felt like I was in complete darkness and that I walked alone. I was keenly aware that it wasn't going to get better any time soon. I had to cut my losses. I had to move forward. I had to recover. But I had no idea how the hell to do it.

I felt like I was stuck on a remote island. I needed a village to see me through, but there was no habitation near me. I was sleep deprived and tired. I was isolated. The darkness made my mind race.

I was isolated, not by choice, but as a matter of self-preservation. I believed I would perish in my remote place because I had little supplies for my existence.

The rarity of my disease kept me from having a vast network of fellow patients, caregivers, and experienced physicians. I didn't have a local community support group. I had little statistical or scientific information on the disease itself and even less information about the recovery process. I knew that no one could come to my aid, which furthered my feelings of loneliness. I didn't know where to send up rescue signals. I feared no one could hear my cries and that I would never be saved.

Good luck.

I was sent home from the Mayo Clinic with a plan for the duration of my medication, but there was no contemporaneous plan with how I would feel along the way or timetables for healing, because that plan doesn't exist. There are no benchmarks for how you are to feel and when. There are no tangible recovery goals. Autoimmune encephalitis does not make you clairvoyant. I had little data from other patients to tell me what's normal and what's not. There's no manual to follow, and there's no self-help book. There's no cure. There's really nothing.

Best wishes to you.

Go forth Jackie. Go forth and heal. Good luck and best wishes.

As my recovery began, I had more questions than I ever had answers. I still don't have all the answers, but I have recovered, and I made it to the one-year date of being autoimmune encephalitis symptom and seizure free! For me, that one year mark gave me the strength and courage to say that I was in remission.

To get there, I resurrected my doubled-edged sword of relentless drive and perseverance through pain. I decided that I would be a survivor in the biggest competition I ever entered. I set my mind to it. I willed myself to beat all odds and rise up.

And I did it.

* * *

As the old proverb goes, "The journey of a thousand miles begins with one single step." To recover from autoimmune encephalitis, you must start out with that single step and attempt to take very small steps forward, day in and day out. You do it because you believe in yourself, and you believe that you can persevere on your road to recovery. You dig deep and know that while the path ahead is less traveled, you have to start down it. The landscape is unknown, and the terrain is bumpy, but the only alternative is to give up, and the consequence of that is a painful life and slow death. So you embark upon your journey, but you start small. And as you get going, you find out that your road takes you one step forward and three steps back. But you put your head down further and go even harder. It's hard. It's scary. It's ugly. It's the hardest thing you will ever have to do in life. You have to rise to the challenge. You can and you will.

CHAPTER 27

In February 2019, at a follow-up neurology appointment at the Mayo Clinic, I saw Dr. McKeon. On that day, I weighed twenty pounds over my normal weight, crept along to walk, and had a hunchback and mustache, all thanks to my steroids. Just like I did time and time again on my recovery road, I broke down. I told him that I felt awful. I was so afraid of everything, and I had lost my career. I felt outgunned by life.

I will never forget how he looked at me with great empathy and compassion and said, "It's a devastating disease, really."

There is no greater word to use when describing autoimmune encephalitis and its aftermath. The struggle of onset is mind blowing, and the struggle of recovery is gut wrenching. It's all devastating.

It is my humble and non-medical opinion, based solely upon my own experience, that the recovery process can be broken down into five main categories of hardship: physical issues, mental health, social problems, issues surrounding your career and livelihood, and overwhelming and debilitating fear.

Healing a sick brain takes more than resting your mind. You also have to heal many parts of your body and spirit. And for me, the actual disease and its treatment led me to suffer from many other medical and mental "collateral issues" that similarly affected these five areas of my life. While there is surely overlap in the categories, each one presents its own unique challenges through healing and recovery.

Another separate and distinct challenge is to understand where you are with your illness and where you are with your recovery. If you're in a stage of active illness, chances are you're in some type of neurological failure or you're in the hospital. Everything is out of your control and left to those around you who love you and care about you. If you're on the outskirts of active illness, chances are you're in survival mode. I often said that, notwithstanding the life of my children and husband, there was nothing of importance to me outside of my own survival. Nothing. And survival was a slow and painful process, one dragging day after another.

Once you have survived, you can focus solely on recovering your injured brain, sick body, and your destroyed life. The recovery phase is long and arduous, and for many, including me, is probably a lifelong process. To some extent, I believe I will always be recovering from this devastating illness.

Once you are in a place of confidence about your recovery, only then can you begin to pick up the shattered pieces of your life and re-build it.

In May 2019, I began telling a few friends and family that I was retiring from practice, and I called my friend Andrea, a well-respected counselor who is skilled in handling crises. I shared with her my sadness and my uncertainty as to my next steps. She replied, "Jackie, first you have to survive. Then you have to recover. And only then can you rebuild."

At that moment, everything around me just stopped, and it all made sense. I had been coping through each stage for nearly a year, but I was never able to articulate the process. I repeated back to her, "SuRvive, Recover, Rebuild. I like that. The three Rs!"

I believe that the three Rs are the key to moving on from autoimmune encephalitis.

CHAPTER 28

SURVIVE

Through June and July, I remained in pure survival mode throughout my Groundhog's days. I felt awful all day, every day. And I wanted to give up—because I hated my life.

For a brief while, I still had just enough drive in me to attempt to keep up some of my old ways, but it was very short-lived. My expectations of my old self weren't realistic.

I was stuck at my home feeling miserable, but I could not disavow all my responsibilities. I still had young children who needed a lot from me, and I was still a 50 percent shareholder in a law firm, although absent. I could not just be sick. I had to be a little more, even when it felt daunting, and I didn't want to do it. It was hard to find any of life's balance against the 99 percent feelings of sickness and hopelessness that plagued me.

If I overdid it or tried to do too much, I became overtired, slept even less, and shook more. With the medication and anxiety, my tremors returned. Doing just about anything, including something as small as going to the grocery store, gave me a great deal of mental exhaustion. I had headaches most days. I did not want to do anything but be left alone at home and lie on the couch. That was all I could do to endure the days.

By early July, I realized that I was shutting down. I knew that people wanted the old Jackie, but I could not deliver that. It frustrated and angered me that people would even expect me to act normal or like my past self so soon after what I had been through.

I didn't want any texts or phone calls because I couldn't handle them. One day, someone rang the doorbell, and I froze. I couldn't answer the front door because I had become overwhelmed. I later found out that it was my close friend Kelly, who stopped by to give me a gift and a hug while he was campaigning for the US Congress. I felt awful when I learned it was him that I ignored because I would have liked to have seen him. But not having notice of who stood outside that front door was just too much for me that day.

On July 14, after a trip to the grocery store with my family, I wrote in my journal: "I still hate being out–I'm unsteady, nervous and feel uncomfortable–but I like planning meals. I still don't like talking to people–I like to be left alone–neighbors mean well."

Sean and I live in a wonderful neighborhood where everyone for blocks knew that I was sick and wanted desperately to help. People around us showed us kindness and generosity, but all of a sudden it became too much for me, and I could hardly bear to see anyone if I set foot outside. I felt selfish, but any type of questions or conversation was too much for me. I rapidly cut out friends and any visitors. The few people left in my social life were my neighbors, and I didn't want to see any of them either.

Each week, Sean put together all my medication in various pill containers because I was unable to do it myself. The stress for him to plan out, refill, precisely cut pills, and distribute all my daily medication was enormous, but I could not have done it. I only trusted *him* to handle my medication. Sean did this for me for over six months.

My eyes remained fuzzy through July, so it was hard to read, but I continued to try. I began by rereading the Harry Potter series and daily Christian devotionals. It wasn't until about August that my eyes started to regain focus and clarity, making it easier to read books.

I persistently struggled with my memory, and it irritated me. After I read my devotionals, I tried to cross-reference the message with the corresponding passage in the Bible, but it was hard to remember the chapter and verse in the seconds that it took me to go from the devotional to the Bible. I also struggled to remember names, especially from when I was getting sick or from current events. Names that were new to me were hard for me to remember. In physical therapy, I struggled to remember which room I was in and would often get turned around coming back from the weight room. If I had a thought on my mind and was even slightly distracted, the thought was instantly gone. I had always prided myself in my amazing memory but felt the defects daily. I was scared that my ability for short-term memory was tarnished and that I would never get it back.

In early July, at my request, Fr. Chris came over to our house to visit me. It was the first time since he saw me in the psychiatric ward. I can't recall much of the specifics of what I told him, but I remember the generality of our conversation. I was nervous, overwhelmed, and looking for God's grace to take the next few steps.

I told him I couldn't handle public settings, and he reassured me that it was acceptable to desire privacy during my healing. He also stressed that it was important for me to ask for help, which was something I notoriously wasn't good at. I heeded both pieces of advice.

I also shared with him my fear that my sickness and recovery were harming my children and that I wasn't being a good mother to them. I couldn't see the effects of my illness on them during my acute onset, but I could see it during recovery. I felt constant guilt that I was burdening them at such a young age.

He assured me that my children would be just fine, that they were resilient. He was correct. But it took me time to see and believe it.

My daughter was very clingy and was sensitive to anything that was even remotely akin to my being sick or hospitalized. She asked a lot of questions about what she thought was my "falling out of bed" to "break my arm," which was actually coined by one of my doctors and stuck around. Rather than trying to explain a brain illness and seizure to a five-year-old, we utilized very simple explanations for a while.

She also needed constant reassurance that I was not going back to the hospital. A television commercial for St. Jude's scared her, and we had to be very careful about anything we said in front of her as it related to my well-being. She continued to sleep with her little brother in his room on a futon Sean had moved in there in May. We knew it made them feel safe, so we allowed it that summer. And to not make them worry more, no matter how hard it was for me, I refused to cry in front of the kids.

All four of our lives entirely stopped. Our daughter was supposed to play t-ball that summer, but we canceled it. We rarely left the house because I didn't want to go anywhere. The most we did was set up a slip and slide for them in the backyard during the afternoon, and every night after dinner we ate popsicles together outside.

As the summer progressed, we tried to prepare our daughter for kindergarten, but I fretted that I wasn't able to do enough with her to fully prepare her for school. She didn't know how to write her name or tie her shoes, and I hadn't seriously discussed "strangers." I lay awake at night and wondered if she would fare well at a large elementary school that first big year because of the chaos that went on at our house.

On July 22, I wrote, "I walked with my head down–felt very annoyed at people, and anyone behind me or with a dog freaks me out!" By that time, I was angry, frustrated, and had completely shut down. I went nowhere, and if I had to go somewhere, I put a hat and sunglasses on. I only went to the mailbox at 6:00 a.m., and I looked straight ahead while walking to not let anyone catch my eye. I checked my email sparingly, called upon hardly anyone, stayed far away from Facebook, and implicitly told the world that I was done with it.

I stayed in that mindset for a long time and didn't apologize for it at all, and neither did my family. I knew if I was going to survive, I had to be selfish. I also knew that the only thing I had to give outside of trying to stay alive every day had to go to my kids, and that was it.

At an appointment with Dr. Dunnigan, he expressed some concern about my becoming a recluse. He told me, "This isn't your personality" and asked me to get out of the house. I heard him out and agreed about my past extroverted nature, but I still argued. I felt like I knew myself best and knew what I needed.

I tried to articulate how I felt and told him there was no way for me to be anything but standoffish and isolated. I couldn't handle questions, looks, noises, distractions, people, crowds, and so much more. He then said, "You struggle with tolerance." His words felt like a bullseye.

I was not convinced that getting out more or trying to socialize past my close family and very limited friends until I was emphatically ready would help. And it felt like my world was divided straight down the middle—those who understood that and those who did not.

On July 31, I journaled a candid view of my life:

> today marks 12 weeks that I've been gone from work—in some ways it feels longer—I do miss SM Law
>
> I still think a lot about the disability claim—probably too much
>
> West Wing has reinspired my love of civics, campaigns, politics & the law
>
> I'm excited for a new job but worry about $ & and the market—have to believe in me & that there's something for me!
>
> I did 2 laps @ 25 mins & 20 mins on the bike—darn knees—still taping
>
> I still feel fatigue, take steps 1 @ a time, some headaches, a little memory issues & speaking is harder at night, when kids are yelling & Sean tries to talk to me (& if TV on or phone) I get distracted, I don't want to listen to music much either, I pay attention when I walk
>
> recovery is a full-time job, calendar appointments, blood sugar, weight, writing my food log, shoulder exercises, ice, heat, snacks, water, timers for pills—all I do.

Time moved slowly, and I was in so much mental and physical pain that I wondered how long I could keep it all up. All I could do was try to enjoy my quiet early mornings, get through the long afternoons, survive dinnertime meltdowns with little kids, and wait desperately to go to bed, only to do it all over again the next day. Just keep swimming, people told me.

Just keep swimming, Jackie.

CHAPTER 29

RECOVER

On August 1, 2018, I wrote: "Holy cow, we made it to August!" My conscious effort to balance my five pillars of recovery slowly began at this time.

Physical Issues

The physical effects I faced during recovery were some of my most obvious problems but were the slightest in gravity. They were also the only ones I felt like I had some control over.

The steroids hurt my joints and my body, and I rapidly felt the terrible physical effects. My movements were slow and deliberate, and I was hunched over when I walked.

I bound my knees and ankles with athletic tape to walk, and I pushed through the heel and shin pain. My knee pain was so great that it woke me up from the small bit of sleep I could get, so I slept in braces. My knees hobbled me, especially up and down our stairs. While in my recliner, I used ice packs and a heating pad nearly all day on my knees, shoulders, neck, and low back.

I also felt the physical effects of addiction to the steroids, which was new to me. Like clockwork every day, I experienced withdrawals as I neared the time to take my next dose. I mostly felt it in my jaw and chest. My jaw clenched and shook and caused me to bite my tongue and lip, and I lost the ability to relax my jaw while at rest. My chest pounded and felt heavy. Once I took the dose of steroids and added in seizure medication in the morning and evening, I was visibly unsteady and became irritable and anxious.

From the time I woke up in the middle of the night until I took my first cocktail of pills at about 6:00 a.m., was the only time that I didn't feel drunk, clumsy, rage, and like I was having a heart attack. From 1:00 a.m. to 4:00 a.m. were my best hours, sometimes the only mentally productive ones I had all day. After I took my first heavy dose of medication in the early morning, the rest of the day was insufferable.

I didn't want any affection from anyone but my children and shared virtually no intimacy with my husband. I didn't want to be touched and couldn't handle anything near my face.

On top of my neurological issues, with my slow movements and inability to move my swollen neck, I couldn't drive.

By late August, my face was puffy, and I had grown a mustache. By October, I had gained so much fluid weight from the steroids that I looked pregnant, and my face looked like it could pop. Deep, ugly stretch marks appeared all over my body, including inside my armpit, where I now have a large scar that looks like I was burned. With my short hair, swollen face, and all the weight gain, I was unrecognizable, even to people who knew me. While out trick or treating with our children, a lawyer I had known for years introduced himself to me. I even had to casually mention Ashley to my friend Senator Heidi Heitkamp when we posed for a photo together, and she seemed shocked to discover that it was *me* she was standing next to.

I felt different and invisible, which was the worst side effect I endured. But as my appearance changed, I didn't hide from the way I looked, nor did I shy away from photographs. It was all part of my illness and was outside of my control. I didn't look like myself, and I didn't like the woman who looked back at me in the mirror. Yet there was nothing I could do to conquer the effects of the steroids. As time went on, I found a way to look through myself in the mirror, and I never believed that the person looking back at me was, in fact, me.

From late June through August, I worked tirelessly to rehabilitate my shoulder, because it was the one tangible thing that I could see in recovery. I started physical therapy with Lesley on June 27, 2018, and she was a true blessing in my life. We really clicked, and she understood the complete picture with me. Until October, Lesley and I spent a few times a week together in therapy, where she stretched me, pushed me, worked with me and allowed me to be sick and sometimes very frustrated. One time, when I was fraught with emotion over my dissolution from the law firm, our entire session consisted of me sobbing and her rubbing my back and talking to me. I didn't like leaving the house, and therapy was painful, but I always looked forward to seeing her during those first two months, and I didn't look forward to seeing anyone.

On July 10, 2018, I saw Dr. Pierce. He informed me that my break wouldn't heal for another four weeks and that I had a Hill-Saks lesion. I learned that it was a permanent dent in my bone, like someone popped a big pocket of bubble wrap inside my shoulder socket. Dr. Pierce was stern that day that I needed to have much more movement than I did at the time, or he would be forced to give me an injection. I did not want an injection, so I rose to his challenge.

I had another appointment with him on August 7, so I aimed to be able to raise my arm to wash my hair and shave my armpit by that morning. I had a long way to go, though, as I was barely rotating my wrist and forearm at the appointment day. The thought of lifting my right arm to 180 degrees and using it in one month felt like climbing Mt. Everest.

For that next month, I worked tirelessly doing shoulder stretches over five times a day, when three to four were ordered, and I was constantly moving. I used sticks, bands, a pulley, a small weight, and my basketball, and started the long and painful process to be functional again. The challenge was unique to me because I had to start moving the shoulder socket that was dislocated and then immobilized while I was also trying to allow the break to heal. The pain was miserable and so were my daily stretches, but my determination, along with heat, ice, and steroids, kept me going.

On August 7, I raised my arm up in front of Dr. Pierce, just after washing my hair and shaving my armpit. I was proud of myself and those around me were too, but, unfortunately, it was the only concrete and quick process that I felt like I made for a year.

I felt a burning desire to attempt to take control of my life. So I devised ways to take my memories back.

After driving by the fire station, I decided I wanted to meet the firemen who had come to my rescue on that fateful May night. So on February 2, 2019, my family took a trip there, and I was able to meet and personally thank Captain Wilke, Mike, and Nathan. Unfortunately, Derek wasn't there.

They were a joy to meet, and because of it I have only a fond appreciation for that crew and not terrors of a night I can't remember.

The experience of the March 26-27, 2018 insomnia-filled trial, along with the music I had downloaded and the potent smell of my car, was an overwhelming memory, and I was sick of it. So on March 26, 2019, I attempted to purge it.

I got in my car and found a country road, far out of town. With the spring air rushing through my windows, I blared Elton John's "I'm Still Standing" over and over as I accelerated my car down the open road. I then stopped at the side of the road and smashed the CDs of the music I made for that moment. I stomped them into the ground while Elton continued to sing "I'm still standing, yeah yeah yeah!"

The experience was powerful, and I felt alive. Yet the smell of my car remains.

Mental Health

When I was released from the hospital and began my treatment, I was shocked that my providers wouldn't allow me to discontinue my anti-depressants and anti-anxiety medication. I didn't believe it was necessary, because, after all, I wasn't mentally ill. I had encephalitis. I didn't think I needed mental health medication.

I quickly learned that treating my mental health was a big piece of my rotating puzzle.

It was challenging because it was all new territory to me. I had endless questions about my mental state: What is a medical issue? What is situational? What is a side effect from medication? What part is my healing brain playing in this? And what is a true mental health issue? I knew that the answers to those complicated questions were far past my paygrade, so I tried to do the best I could with the skills I was equipped with.

I relied upon my own judgment, insight I had from working with mental health professionals at work, and advice from Mom. I continued to treat with Stephanie Macdonald, and I stayed on medication for over one year.

I was down and grieving. And virtually everything made me anxious. Every emotion and feeling was compounded by another. My anxiety kept me isolated, which contributed to my sadness. My nerves led to physical effects like chest pain and shaking. And my medication caused psychiatric side effects. I was so irritable I wanted to explode. My brain worked at a slow pace, which frustrated me. And I felt triggers everywhere. Sights, sounds, smells, dates, and flashbacks took me back to the spring when life began to unravel, and it was traumatizing.

I used a variety of coping mechanisms to try to have some semblance of a balanced mental state. By far, what was most important to my well-being was my vast support system that included Sean, Mom, my family, and some close friends. In a close second place was my writing. I diligently wrote in a daily journal to express my feelings. I wrote on my CaringBridge site, which allowed people to hear from me and send me support. I even wrote nastygrams that no one else saw. I wasn't comfortable with my spoken word, so it was better to express myself in writing.

I faithfully exercised and frequently rested. Time I spent in motion helped clear my thoughts and release negativity. While working out, even though it was of low intensity, I felt empowered. Rest recharged my brain, body, and spirit. When I was able to rest, I was fresher, felt more purpose, and had hope. I was happiest while exercising and after I slept.

I spent a lot of time in deep thought, reflection, and prayer. Each day I read daily Christian devotionals, the Bible, and prayed the rosary. I also had the support of three close priest friends whom I was able to confide in. They visited my home to talk with me and frequently checked in on me, which was all very comforting.

As time went on and music became less distracting to me, I found it to be very therapeutic. It became another way for me to express my varying emotions. I listened to sad songs, happy songs, inspirational songs, and dark songs. I mostly repeated the songs, "Let It Be" and "The Boxer." And, I added in Elton John's "I'm Still Standing" and "Hall of Fame" as much as I could.

I frequently used the mantra #StebbinsStrong. It became my signature. I even had shirts made for my family. I told myself that #StebbinsStrong meant that I could and would overcome all the challenges I faced and that I would heal. When people repeated it back to me, I knew that they believed in me too.

I had to stay strong for my family. I could not allow myself to slip into the deep, dim places of sadness, bitterness, resentment, and anger. In some of my dark times, I wondered if my family would be better off if I were dead, but those were very fleeting thoughts because I knew my family was better with me present and healthy. I never felt suicidal, nor did I ever want to harm myself, but I was admittedly very down for a long time. I also felt a lot of guilt that was hard to get over.

As much as I tried to repeat Dr. Z's words in my mind that it was not my fault, all the self-blame and guilt did not instantly vanish. The persistent feelings of failure, regret, and obsessions about what if I had just done this, or that, plagued me for a long time. And because I will never understand how or why I had autoimmune encephalitis, it wasn't a thought that I could easily put to rest. It took an enormous amount of patience and grieving to rid myself of the feelings and to reframe my thoughts into ones that were healthy and positive.

I tried to exude and feel copious amounts of positivity. When I spoke publicly on my CaringBridge page, or when I did encounter people at my home or through electronic means, I put on the bravest face I could muster and stayed upbeat. I knew that people would follow my cue. The more positive I stayed, the more positive they would feel about my situation.

I tried to look at life through a lens of perspective and remind myself that I was still very lucky in a lot of ways. Life's struggles were everywhere. I was not alone in illness or sorrow. And as much as I hated the saying "It could be worse," I often repeated it, and made a conscious effort to believe it.

I did the best I could, but it was admittedly very hard to sort through it all and build back a healthy mind. I contemplated counseling during the first year but chose not to pursue it. It felt like another chore and a big burden when everything was still so fresh. I expressed a wide array of emotions each day and cried a lot, mostly when no one was looking. I liked it better that way.

It took years for my mental health to finally catch up to me and for me to let my guard down. And only then was I ready for a counselor.

Social Problems

My social issues were challenging and overwhelming and caused me the most agony and hurt. In hindsight, it's because my disease is so unrelatable. Overwhelmingly, people don't have family members or friends with autoimmune encephalitis. Most of the people around me had never even heard of it, including those in the medical profession. I hoped that people in my wider circle would understand. I wanted them to get what I was going through and be able to communicate with me. And hands down, most people tried their best to realize, relate, and offer me help. But the ones who didn't try or didn't understand caused me heartache.

Hardly a month after I was out of the hospital, people began to ask me and my family if I was back to work yet, which felt like a slap in the face. Day to day I could barely function through routine tasks, so no, I was not back to work at my law firm. I was not working toward million-dollar goals, for over sixty hours a week, six days a week, and tackling complicated legal issues. Even a year into my recovery, I became agitated when people asked me if I had returned to work.

The social issue was intertwined with my changing physical appearance, my mental health issues, and my lack of a job. It compounded and swirled into agonizing fear. My mood and personality were different. I knew I wasn't myself, and I could see when others realized that I wasn't the "old Jackie." I knew I couldn't meet expectations in conversations, and it was nearly impossible to go out into public, so I felt the further isolation and removal from life.

I didn't look good or feel good, so I didn't feel good about myself. I didn't have it in me to dress nicely and engage in a social setting. I was self-conscious about my injured and ill brain, so I further shied away from people and crowds because I worried about what people were saying or thinking. And worse yet, I knew that people were questioning whether my brain worked by watching my thoughts, speech, and memory, so I became even more paranoid. I shut down because the idea of any sort of interaction was too much. So I was left to my own devices to heal and to get through the days, and it was awful.

Sean and my family were very open about my recluse status and unapologetically told others that I needed it to survive. Past my posts on CaringBridge, there wasn't much public about me. If I did interact with people, I was honest with them that it was challenging for me to do so, and the time period was limited. Most people understood that I needed time to heal, and we continued to tell people that I would eventually return to "me" status but that it was going to take a lot of time. And that's what it took, a lot of time.

Little by little, I began to return to walks during regular hours of the day, chats with neighbors, phone calls with friends, and I began to leave off my hat and sunglasses when I went into public. It took me over a year to return to settings with groups of people or where more interaction would be desired from me. I didn't feel comfortable going out for a meal with my husband or with friends for a year. When I went to church for the first time again on Christmas Eve in 2018, I felt nervous, overwhelmed, and out of place. I didn't return to regular participation in church until well after one year.

Huge crowds of people were not in the cards, so I gave up my tickets to see Elton John at Madison Square Garden, with Mom, on November 9, 2018. I can specifically point to the worst date of my recovery—it was that day. I cried myself to sleep that night, and when Sean tried to comfort me, I told him, "Go away and leave me alone."

I also gave up my tickets to see his farewell concert in Denver, with Sean, over my birthday in 2019. By that time, I was numb to the pain and knew that his show went on without me, his biggest fan, in attendance.

The worst part about social situations was when I could tell people were afraid of me and afraid of what they were going to find when they came to my house. Some of it passed with time as word got out that I was getting better and when people saw me or heard from me. I can still tell when people are sizing me up and questioning my intelligence or personality, but it doesn't bother me anymore because I've accepted that it's part of my strange and rare illness. I don't believe I have to prove myself to others. I'm comfortable with the facts of my illness and my new life.

After I was about two years away from my onset, I wasn't noticeably different from the way I was before. I'm very lucky to be able to say that. Many autoimmune encephalitis survivors do not seem to share in my same good fortune.

Outside of my not returning to the practice of law and my outlook on life because of my near-death experience, I'm the same old Jackie. A little more cautious and a lot more tired, but still… Jackie.

Career and Livelihood

The loss of my career as a lawyer and all that went with it gave me some of the worst days that I ever had during recovery. It was always raw and emotional for me, but it was something that I had little control over. I could not return to work and had to rely solely upon my disability insurance coverage, which is a stressful process, even for a lawyer. If there was a hiccup in my disability insurance, I wasn't going to be able to do a damn thing about it except sell everything I owned and relocate my family to live with my parents.

The fear of the future and the magnitude of my losses left me nearly debilitated most days. It also compounded the problems with my already fragile state and set off the chain reaction from mental to physical issues.

I struggled to keep bitterness and anger from engulfing me. All my years of planning, all my hard work, and all of my dreams were taken from me in an instant, without any notice. Ken tallied a final number for me one day, what I would have made by age sixty-five. A concrete number placed upon my financial losses was like the last nail in my coffin.

Although I can calculate the tangible loss of income, I'll never be able to calculate the cumulative losses I've endured, from the loss of my career, to the loss of my business, to the loss of my dreams.

My career as a trial lawyer and the Stebbins Mulloy Law Firm no longer exist. On July 31, 2019, ten years to the date since I began as an attorney in Bismarck, I retired from the practice of law. It was a good run, but all good things must come to an end. Or so they say.

Fear

For over a year, I had unbearable worries about what had happened to me and what could possibly happen next. I feared the past, present, and future. All the other issues and challenges I faced led back to this one.

My mental state, my physical limitations, unfair social expectations, and the loss of my livelihood all left me with a tremendous amount of uncertainty. And because I felt like I was an island, I always had more questions than I had answers from reputable sources. *What's next? Am I going to die? Has my life been shortened because of this illness? Will I be "sick" for the rest of my life? Does my brain work like it used to? Am I permanently disabled? Will I go bankrupt? How long does it take to recover? What does recovery look like for me? Do I need to have round-the-clock caregivers? Will I ever have a career again? Have I lost my professional connections? Have I lost my abilities? Do I have a different personality? What's going to happen to my children?* The questions were endless, and it was a challenge to not let them drag me down through my long days.

I nervously faced my own mortality for an entire year, and it did not help that I had lost many loved ones around me during that year. Chelsea died from her cancer on July 7, 2018. On January 6, 2019, I tragically lost a law school classmate, Rachel, to cancer, after we had just caught up in the two preceding months. And on March 10, 2019, I lost Judge Anderson because of cancer. I had lost other friends and acquaintances along the way, but the loss of these three women devastated me. I only took comfort in all the conversations I was able to have with each of them before their untimely passing.

On top of the personal losses, I saw stories on encephalitis threads and blogs about people who had died from my disease. My fragile health and mortality weighed on me for a long time. But I realized that I had to face my fears, and I had to live. I had to go on amidst the horrors that my disease brought on me and others. I finally refused to live in a state of worry and accepted every day as it came to me.

I became the little girl in the photograph and looked over my shoulder to see the light.

* * *

To face my fears while recovering, I expected very little from myself, especially while surviving and during the early stages of recovery. As I grew in my recovery, I relished the little victories to gain confidence and alleviate some of my fretting. And I only set achievable and practical goals.

I took pleasure in the small things: the first time I picked-up my children; the first children's book I read them; my first out-of-town drive; the first time I put on a suit; when I got back down to my target weight; when people told me I looked like myself or sounded like the old Jackie; when I told a joke in a group and people laughed; when I could take stairs one at a time; and for the first time after fifteen years, when I put on my rollerblades and cruised around the neighborhood. The more I accomplished, even when it was a small feat, the less I feared. And the more I cared for my physical, mental, and social well-being, I became less concerned about an untimely death.

For one year, I faced and overcame some serious medical fears. I made a total of four trips to the Mayo Clinic in 2018-2019, and each trip made me nervous that something else was wrong with me. In November 2018, I was referred to an endocrinologist for concerns about my parathyroid hormone. That visit ended up with my being diagnosed with severe osteoporosis. Also in November, I underwent a breast biopsy and found out nearly immediately that I didn't have breast cancer! In February 2019, I saw a gastroenterologist for concerns about my colitis. I hardly met with the doctor for a few minutes before he asked me if I had ever been screened for celiac disease. The initial bloodwork came back positive, so I returned a few weeks later in March to undergo an upper endoscopy to confirm the diagnosis. And sure enough, I had celiac disease.

I encountered plenty of other issues that I chalked up to my health and medication wigging out my body. I cracked two teeth from all the time I clenched my jaws and when I suffered from withdrawals. I have TMJ, and I'm still learning how to relax my jaws. My hair stopped growing, and a lot of it fell out. I have cataracts in both eyes. In December 2019, I had to have a large part of both of my big toenails cut out. The irony was not lost on us that when we left Mayo in June 2018, Sean joked on a CaringBridge post that I had been screened from head to toe, the only exception being my toenails.

I appreciated steroids for saving my brain, but I hated them because they wreaked havoc on my body. Through my hard work and diligent efforts, I narrowly escaped a diabetes diagnosis. I exercised, tested my blood sugar daily, and maintained a strict diet. I was diagnosed with high blood pressure, but with medication and my efforts it came down as I reduced my steroid intake. I kept a detailed food and exercise journal for over a year. I drastically altered my eating to a strict gluten-free diet to reverse my celiac disease, and it helped my overall health immensely. And because Dr. Dunnigan told me to eat a banana every day while I was on steroids, I religiously adhered to that. I kept my food journal for four hundred twenty-eight days, and out of those days I only missed eating a banana a handful of times.

I felt an overwhelming sense of pride one day when Dr. Froelich told me that a large part of my recovery and improved health was because of my efforts. While I believe I benefited immensely from the wonderful medical care I received, I also believe that my hard work in controlling the little things I had control over served me well.

REBUILD

Life went on and I went with it. My kids bounced back from the trauma they endured from my illness, and they're perfectly healthy and well-adjusted children. My daughter started kindergarten and thrived there. She loved school, and I had plenty of time to work with her on her writing, reading, tying her shoes, and never talking to strangers. My son was eventually potty trained and sent off to preschool, where he also flourished. And Sean, my stalwart hero, returned to the job he enjoyed before we had children, a communications director for a non-profit, so he could begin to rebuild his career and provide our family with health insurance.

We stayed in our same house and have not yet made any major changes in our lives. We're still mindful of the future, but we've learned to let a lot go. We do our best to enjoy every today and remember that our lives are happily worth living because the alternative for us was my untimely death. I'll continue to endure any curve balls life throws at me if it means I stay on earth with my family.

Through all the ups and downs, all the small victories and set-backs, I made it to May 26, 2019. I was seizure free and off seizure medication! I was in remission from autoimmune encephalitis!

My family celebrated that Memorial Day weekend by camping at the lake. That morning, I sat on a picnic table by myself, looking out over the water and pondering my past accomplishments and future dreams. I have survived the worst. The terrifying thoughts I had while lying awake at night in my bed did come true. I lost my job, my career, my livelihood, and my law firm. I lost even more than I had worried about. I lost my mind, my memory, my body, my hair, and so much else. But I fought back out of what felt like the black hole of infinity. I was alive and my brain worked. And even though I was still recovering, I was finally ready and excited to start slowly rebuilding my life.

That night, I wrote in my journal "The world is waiting—something big is for me." I started writing this book the next day.

PART IV – A NEW HOPE

You don't need a prayer
And there's no price to ask why
Well, sometimes you'll find an answer in the sky.

"Answer in the Sky" by Elton John

CHAPTER 30

By the end of May 2019, I looked a lot more like myself and had lost almost all the twenty-seven pounds of fluid weight I had gained. In June, I put long extensions in my hair and felt like I looked the best I had looked since early 2018. By late July, I weighed less than my target weight, was rollerblading, swimming, and biking a few times a week, loved my fake hair, and began to accept that I was forced to retire from the practice of law. The end of the recovery process was nearer, and the beginning of rebuilding Jackie was on the horizon. For the first time in a really long time, life made some sense to me.

One early August morning, my friend Jon helped me put together my work desk in my new office space that Ken and his wife Alison allowed me to use, so I could maintain a professional address for my Bar license. We set up my desk, my bookcase, and my file cabinet. I took a look around at the framed diplomas and the familiar light-brown finish on my furniture, and even though I had no idea what my future held, it all seemed to be coming together a little at a time. I had a whole new life ahead and, while it was all still a little scary, a little excitement started to brew inside of me.

That evening, on Sean's thirty-eighth birthday, we ate cupcakes with the kids and Kathy to celebrate. Shortly thereafter, I said that I had to take some rotten apples back to the grocery store, but that was really a cover-up. I wanted to buy a pregnancy test. I hadn't had my period for a long time while on steroids, but it eventually returned. That day, I had a strange and nervous feeling that it wasn't coming again. I couldn't believe it could be true, that I could be pregnant, but I decided to take a test to have peace of mind. After all my body had been through, it had to be a moot point.

In my frenzy, I thought back to the fall of 2017, when my life felt underwater, and we decided to take permanent action on the completeness of our family. Our dream of having three children when we first talked about getting married was just not meant to be, so we knew we were done at two healthy kids. We then scheduled a surgery.

Yet the unexplainable happened the night before. We questioned our decision, even though we believed our family was complete, and we were too old and tired to have another baby. But we couldn't say absolutely never. We couldn't rule out the possibility of another baby. We talked about the joy of once again seeing that brand new, tiny face in the delivery room. We thought about the fun of another little personality in our home. It was an odd paradox, but we both felt comfortable with our midnight decision to not say never again. And then we canceled the appointment and moved on with our busy life.

I raced home from the store and hurried to take the test. I remained fixated on the line when it came through rapidly and clearly. I was pregnant. I stared at the test in awe, and as one million thoughts raced through my mind, I almost passed out from shock. Not saying never again left open the possibility that it could happen. And now it was happening.

Right after my jolt, Sean and I went on a walk with the kids, and through strange eye contact and hand gestures Sean found out we were pregnant. I could tell by his face that he was as shocked as I was. All he could utter was, "Oh my God." I couldn't even say anything good or bad, because I was in complete disbelief. I called Mom, and she too struggled for words because she couldn't believe it either. She even repeated that after all my body had been through, there was no way I could be pregnant. But I was.

I called Dr. Froelich while sitting in my closet. She was excited for me. She said, "This pregnancy is going to be the best thing for you. It will put you into remission and keep you there. This is just what you need to reset your body."

I went through dates with her and continued to say, "How did this happen? It doesn't even make sense."

She offered a beautiful response... "Some things we just can't explain."

For the next few months, not only could I not explain it, the reality was hard for me to accept. I felt like I was back in crisis mode, but now it wasn't just my health to worry about, it was the health of my baby. Mom and Sean were also very worried about the health of both of us.

I underwent tests in the clinic the day after I found out, and the constant tests and appointments with my regular OB, Dr. Jill Steinle, and a high-risk OB, Dr. Ana Tobiasz, continued throughout the duration of the pregnancy. My high risks were pages long, so it all seemed unimaginable that it could work out for the best for either of us. I was thirty-five years old, which is a geriatric age in pregnancy. I was still recovering from a rare and serious brain illness, along with having many other active collateral medical issues, including a new autoimmune blood clotting disorder. And I was still on some prescription medication during conception.

Dr. Tobiasz gave me the little bit of reassurance that she could so early on, and after that I held my breath and tried desperately to keep moving forward. Mom, Sean, and I were all back at it again, hoping and praying for a good outcome, when we had little control over what would lie ahead.

* * *

I tried to take life just one day at a time, but the pregnancy had me so overwhelmed and scared that I struggled to function. A surprise pregnancy was not something I had ever felt before, and it came with some of the strongest feelings I've ever experienced. Sean's emotions and outlook were very similar to mine. We felt a constant preoccupation with the unknown. I tried to keep myself as busy as I could with the household and the kids, but the extreme emotions seeped out of me. And I was still so tired from my illnesses. My mind just kept buzzing: *How can I possibly incubate, deliver, and take care of a baby?*

My first important ultrasound appointment was during the eleventh week. Both Sean and Mom accompanied me to the clinic. We also went through a genetic counseling class that day, but Sean and I declined to perform any genetic tests. The baby was ours, and we held all hope that she would be healthy.

After the ultrasound, Dr. Tobiasz returned with all good news—the baby looked healthy! We all released a little air that day but continued to feel some alarm until the twenty-week ultrasound.

In between those appointments, I believed I suffered a miscarriage, but the doctors discovered that I had a hemorrhage above my uterus. For a few days, I believed that all I was coming to accept was lost.

At the twenty-week appointment, Dr. Tobiasz again happily reported that the baby looked perfect, and she was developing and growing at a healthy rate. I then let out the largest exhale of my life, and we had a gender reveal party with pink balloons for our excited kids, grandparents, and Lacie, who was back to holding my hand during my time of need.

After that successful appointment, we finally felt obligated to share our news with the general public. I can't say that I was comfortable sharing it, because I still had so many emotions going through me. And when I had told family and a few close friends, I usually ended up crying. Deep down, I also questioned what others were going to say to me, given the status of my life. I assumed people would judge us.

Overall, the news seemed to be just as monumental to others as it was to us. The reactions I received were at drastic ends of the spectrum. People either burst out laughing with excitement and cheer and noted that a surprise and impossible pregnancy was not unthinkable with me, or they stared at me, tears welled up in their eyes, and they genuinely asked me if I was going to be okay. No one offered harsh criticism or judgment. Everyone was happy for us. Overall, the words "blessing" and "miracle" were most often used.

As time went on, I not only accepted the pregnancy, I embraced it. I thought back to 2017 when we said, "Never say never." I thought about the mother's ring I made myself long ago that had my two childrens' birthstones on the sides and a diamond in the middle. A diamond, the birthstone for April, when our baby girl was due. I believed it was divine intervention, and a beautiful ending to an otherwise tragic story for me. I felt all the women whom I lost while I was sick watching over me. Chelsea, Rachel, and Sonna took care of me and the baby. They all knew how fragile life could be and from their little signs along the way, especially Rachel's "white light," I felt their heavenly presence and comfort.

It was the end of my story and the start of a fresh beginning. It was something special that I hadn't planned on in my new life. Dr. Froelich's words kept running through my mind… "You have an ending for your book!"

* * *

Beginning on March 15, 2020, because of the Covid-19 pandemic, the state of North Dakota went under an executive order, which, among other things, shut down schools. I began homeschooling my kids, and we sheltered in place. We questioned whether Sean could even be present with me in the delivery room. It was a scary thought, but I braced myself for it to be a reality. It all seemed to be just my bad luck, but this time the whole world was having a fit of bad luck.

In the cool, wee hours of an April morning, Sean and I arrived at the hospital and entered the Emergency Room, the same one I occupied after my seizure. We both wore N-95 masks while passing through. We feared the virus, memories from our past stay in the hospital, and all of my high risks. But the worries all quickly subsided as I delivered a perfectly healthy baby girl, who had a beautiful little face.

Her initials are AE, just like my illness. We thought she had enough of a back story, but she added some more. She was born on April Fools' Day in the midst of a worldwide pandemic. She's everything we prayed for in our darkest days.

She is hope.

Epilogue

I try not to ask *why me?* because I believe that maybe there was a good reason for me to contract autoimmune encephalitis. I was given many gifts in my life, most notably the gift to use my spoken word to advocate, going way back to when I would negotiate with my parents as a child. With the good fortune I had to secure a liberal arts education and attend law school, I was able to refine my gift for the written word too. And for nearly a decade, I honed my advocacy skills as a trial lawyer. With my talent and the hard work I put into my life for the years before autoimmune encephalitis, I laid the foundation to be a motivational speaker. I built the career, and now I have the story, just like Mom told me I needed all those years ago. It is as if my whole life was destined for this end. All of my struggles won't be for naught; they will be for something bigger than me.

My legs still ache. They are continuous reminders of the way I expected too much of my body and the pain I caused. But I've forgiven myself for it. My shoulder often hurts and is a not-so-subtle reminder of a grand mal seizure that could have taken my life. My weary hip and knee joints are the remnants of the steroids that saved my brain. Yet all the hurt reminds me of how I crawled through hell to beat autoimmune encephalitis. It is a reminder of my strength and what I have overcome.

I'm frequently asked how I did it. How was I so resilient in the face of destruction? In my opinion, I had nowhere else to go. I never wanted to believe that where I was at was it. I believed that each day was a restart and that I had a choice to either accept the bleak terms or to get better. That decision was mine to make every day, and it's still a conscious daily decision that I have to make. I once heard the saying "Pain is unavoidable, but suffering is optional." I have felt my fair share of pain, but I try to avoid suffering.

If I could change it all, would I? And would I go back and do things differently? An easy answer is… yes. I would go back and tell my sixteen-year-old self that she can achieve her wildest dreams without self-inflicting so much pain and pressure. I would tell the twenty-five-year-old me that she can become a great lawyer in her own right, but that she needs to focus on self-care, along with work. I would tell thirty-year-old me that mental health isn't weakness, and little me that there are ways to cope with worry and perfection. I could go back and never endure the tragedy of autoimmune encephalitis and the agony I know it caused others, mostly my family.

But even if I could change the past, I'm not sure I would. Without my life's experiences and my personality traits, I would not be the person I am today. Even though my drive and expectations led me to pursue unreasonable demands of myself, they also combined with hard work and persistence to achieve lofty goals. And without my instincts, I could not have recovered from autoimmune encephalitis the way I did.

Overall, I think it's more important to learn from the past, rather than wish to change it. I have learned from my past and will use my knowledge for a better me and a better future. Through all the pain, I have found meaning, hope, and healing. I have found me… a more mindful me.

I no longer worry about life in the future. I've spent an inordinate amount of time in my life worrying. I worried about what would happen to me, what would be my "thing in life," and what would be my struggle. I found out. Before she died, Rachel wrote, "You're stronger than you think," and I believe it. You can make some plans and use good judgment where you will, but overall, the constant in life is that it's going to change. You have to change with it. Life could again take me by surprise, but all I need to know is that I believe in me, and many around me do too.

I believe that unfair things happen to good people. When faced with adversity, you have to continue to move forward, even if it's in a new direction. And while you're moving on, you have to believe that things are going to turn out all right in the end. Time and time again, I go back to the Julian of Norwich quote, "All things shall be well, and all things shall be well, and all manner of things shall be well."

My resilience mostly came from the strength of those around me. They believed in me and told me I would rise again, so who was I not to believe that I would make a comeback? I have admittedly had dark days. But, thankfully, I overcame those days and stayed on the path to sunshine. I told myself I had conquered plenty in the past, and I had to do it all over again, whether I wanted to or not. And I did it.

I kept the faith, and together, Sean and I kept our humor. One day during recovery, Sean noted that we had failed to have an "autoimmune encephalitis action plan." We laughed hysterically at the notion. We'll do better next time, I guess. And until then, we will use our humor to wade through the difficult past and continue on into the future.

I have been very honest through my struggles. My whole life is now down on paper, in various CaringBridge entries, blog posts, news stories, and this book. I believe that the trick to dealing with a chronic illness is to be honest. You must be completely honest with yourself. You also have to be as honest with others as you can when the timing is right for you. Honesty is allowing yourself to grieve your losses, especially the loss of you. It's repeatedly going through the five stages of grief and back and never apologizing for it. And it's knowing that true and radical acceptance takes time. Clinging to my honesty and cherishing the gratitude I felt flowing out of me were two of my most important recovery virtues.

I believe that everything I do is for my children. All that I endured was for them. I still listen to the song "Hall of Fame," but I don't care if others know my name. I'm still convinced that the song is for my children and all I want for them. I resolve to keep going, no matter what, one foot in front of the other, for those three precious beings. I want them to find their own halls of fame, and I want to be there in the audience cheering when they do.

After I retired from practice, a friend told me that she believed it had brought out the worst in me and wished me a good riddance from the only professional life I knew. I loved my career, and my job gave me great dignity. I believed it was my calling. But maybe the practice of law wasn't the best for my personality and body, no matter the resumé I built and respect and notoriety I earned. It is quite possible that my dream wasn't good for me. Maybe the dream was best to be chased and not lived.

Or maybe it was the perfect fit for me, and life delivered me a staggering blow. My character served me well. I helped people who needed me. If I changed the world for the better by helping one person, then I accomplished what I set out to do so long ago. My legacy as a lawyer lives on, and I'm proud of that. And as a beloved colleague, Kim, told me on the day I publicly announced my leaving practice, "Jackie, you may be retired, but you will always be a trial lawyer. It is in your soul!" And I still have my license to practice law, often saying that the devil himself will have to pry it out of my cold, dead hands.

Overall, the good news is that whether the practice of law was good for me or bad, it really doesn't matter, because my work as a trial lawyer is in a past life, and I have been given a new life, with a new outlook.

I want to lead a life with no fear and no regrets. It's that much easier to move forward, keep the faith, and find happiness when you don't regret the past and fear the future. I now believe that no matter what, autoimmune encephalitis just happened to me, and there wasn't a damn thing anyone could have done about it. The more I believe that it wasn't precipitated by me, the easier it is to accept that it happened to me.

Am I on the Yellow Brick Road or off? Is my story one of defeat where I had to walk away, or is it one of triumph? I know the answer that I have in my heart, although I don't know how others would answer for me. I'll allow them to judge how I've handled this disease and its aftermath—that's really past me. I'm at peace with where I've been and where I'm going. After all, Elton John, the man whom I look to for inspiration, said it best in song long ago, "I'm still standing—yeah yeah yeah!"

I'm still standing, that's all that matters.

And I'm not done yet. I still have a way to go before I reach the top.

Acknowledgments

It takes a village. I'm so thankful for the villagers who helped save me and believed that I could write this book.

To Mom and Sean, for repeatedly re-creating the story for me. To my children, who allowed me countless hours so they could call me an author.

To the team at Calumet Editions, for making my dream a reality: Ian Graham Leask, Gary Lindberg, Rick Polad, and Stevie Ada Klaark.

To Clay Jenkinson; Jack Weinstein and Kim Donehower; Kate Vogl and my spring 2021 Loft writing class; Maria Burns Ortiz; Wolfgang Wright, Tina Holland, and Tony Bender for all the help and hard work of turning me into an author. To Sue Skalicky, Dr. Ava Easton, Christopher Pieske, Esq., and Rebecca Binstock, Esq., for their reviews and support.

To my "Chosen Family," the heroes of this story: Lacie Van Orman; Ashley R. Heitkamp, Esq.; Betsy A. Elsberry, Esq.; Micheal A. Mulloy, Esq.; Erica Johnson; Fr. Chris J. Kadrmas; Stephanie Macdonald, N.P.; Dr. Ralph T. Dunnigan; Captain Matt Wilke; Mike Miller; Nathan Kron; Derek Fladland; Dr. Vivek K. Vadehra; Dr. Denise MacDonald; Dr. Joy Froelich; Dr. Andrew McKeon; Dr. Anastasia Zekeridou; Mac J. Schneider, Esq., Roger & Dorothy Thomas; Kathy Wachter; Derek Lyson; Lesley Westin; Andrea Martin; Ken and Alison Krumm; Dr. Jill Steinle; Dr. Ana Tobiasz, and Dr. Juliana Nevland.

To my family, for their unending love and support: Sean Arithson, K, K, and AE, Jack and Colleen Stebbins, Kathy Arithson, Mike Stebbins (and family), David Stebbins, Shelly Watson (and family), Kelly Slagter (and family), Ruth Kline, Robert and Nicole Klemisch, Nola and Gene Helm, and to so many other aunts, uncles, and cousins. To all my friends and neighbors who encouraged me and believed in me. And to the complete strangers who brightened my life. To countless medical professionals in Bismarck, ND, and Rochester, MN, whose names I can't possibly know or remember.

To Susannah Cahalan for bravely writing *Brain on Fire*. And to the Autoimmune Encephalitis Alliance and the Encephalitis Society for their important work.

About the Author

Jackie M. Stebbins was living her dream as a nationally recognized family law, criminal defense, and civil litigator. But Stebbins's career as a lawyer abruptly ended in May, 2018, when she was diagnosed with a rare brain illness, autoimmune encephalitis. Stebbins persevered to make a remarkable recovery and turned herself into an author and motivational speaker. Stebbins is the author of the *JM Stebbins* blog and host of the *Brain Fever* podcast. Stebbins's side hustle includes raising three lovely children with her wonderful husband, Sean, in Bismarck, North Dakota, and in her leisure time she can be found reading, trying to be funny, and aqua jogging.

Made in the USA
Middletown, DE
13 May 2022